Family Systems Activity Book

Clive Hazell

Bloomington, IN   Milton Keynes, UK

AuthorHouse™
1663 Liberty Drive, Suite 200
Bloomington, IN 47403
www.authorhouse.com
Phone: 1-800-839-8640

AuthorHouse™ UK Ltd.
500 Avebury Boulevard
Central Milton Keynes, MK9 2BE
www.authorhouse.co.uk
Phone: 08001974150

First published by AuthorHouse 5/18/2006

ISBN: 1-4259-1962-6 (e)
ISBN: 1-4259-1504-3 (sc)

Library of Congress Control Number: 2006900488

Printed in the United States of America
Bloomington, Indiana

This book is printed on acid-free paper.

Dedication and Acknowledgements

This book is dedicated to my wife, Rosalinda, my children and everyone in my ever-extending family. I would also like to thank the many teachers I had at Reading University, Northwestern University and the Institute for Juvenile Research, Chicago who introduced me to the systems way of thinking. Thanks to the many students at DeVry University, The School of the Art Institute of Chicago and the Illinois School of Professional Psychology, who helped mould this book with their helpful comments and feedback. Thanks, as always to Marylin Hallett of Michigan Avenue Office Services for excellent work and my gratitude goes out to Shawna Foose and Diana Semmelhack for their useful critique. I am also grateful to Victoria Hazell for her design ideas.

Contents

Introduction

This book focuses on the internal dynamics of the family. Families are extremely important to human beings. It is hard to imagine life without a family, and perhaps even those who claim they have no family, have, in fact, an "imaginary family" in their minds, to which they belong and in which they participate. It is inside the family that we find much of what is meaningful in our lives and where we do much of our psychological growth. Not only is the family important, it is also extremely complex, insofar as it performs many vital functions for humans. This book will attempt to take the reader through the many facets of the family to lay bare its anatomy and its functioning. At the end, perhaps the reader will have a better understanding of the dynamics of family life.

This book will attempt to draw together the complex threads running together through the family. First, the approach involves the use of "systems thinking." The meaning and the implications of this will be spelled out in the early part of the book. Second, the family is a place where biological, psychological and social development takes place. The family itself goes through developmental phases. Thus there follows a section on biopsychosocial development and its relationship to the family.

Families are deeply affected by culture. Thus there will follow a section that opens up this realm, which examines the ways in which the set of beliefs about behavior that are learned and shared in the "cultural surround" can affect the family. It is my basic assumption that families have an unconscious life. Thus, there is a section delineating some basic unconscious processes that operate in families. Many of the unconscious processes that operate in families operate across generations (sometimes many generations). There is therefore a chapter dealing with intergenerational effects and some examination of the intergenerational transmission of trauma.

All of my work is influenced by Dabrowski's theory of positive disintegration. To my awareness, at the time of going to print, this hierarchical model of human development has not been systematically linked to the understanding of family systems. Thus, a chapter is devoted to the application of Dabrowski's theory to the understanding of family dynamics. Next we turn to the topic of love, its many twists and turns and different forms. Finally there are sections on sexual orientation and gender in the family.

This book uses many case studies, involves the study of several movies on the family, and will ask you, from time to time to look inside yourself or to interview others to find out more. At the end of the book, there is a fifteen-week journal, with spaces for you to fill out. This is aimed at helping you gain further insight into families, your own assumptions and expectations and perhaps to give you some understanding of your own family.

CHAPTER 1
Families as Systems

A. What is a system?

This book assumes that families operate as systems. The term "system" has reached the status of a cliché. What does it mean, especially when we apply it to families?

This chapter will describe some of the formal abstract properties of systems, outlining some of the rules by which systems operate, and then show that we can gain a great deal of insight into the way families work if we apply some of these ways of systems thinking to families. First, "What is a system?"

A system is a set of OBJECTS, having ATTRIBUTES, linked together in a NETWORK, through which there are FLOWS.

Thus we might view a family as a set of objects (probably a good place to start here is with the people comprising the family, although we could use any other set of family "objects," for example, "parents" and "children" or "males" and "females"). These people have attributes or qualities—age, health, education, values, traits, history and so on. These people are joined by a multiplicity of networks—verbal communication, money, favors, information, non-verbal communication, gift exchange, kinship, physical contact, sexual contact, telephone, email and so on. Each of these networks has an array of flows along them. Sometimes the flow is two-way, sometimes one way, sometimes equal in both directions, sometimes unequal, as when, say a parent talks to a child but does not listen. Sometimes the flow is heavy, as between two individuals who communicate intensely and regularly, and sometimes the flow is very thin, as between two individuals who rarely communicate.

Similar variation can be found in all four of the elements of a system. There may be many or few objects in a system (people may enter and leave the family). Networks can be very complex and interconnected or very sparse and threadbare.

Figure 1 gives a diagrammatic representation of a family system. In it there are four individuals, mother, father, daughter and son. The diagram shows the amount of verbal conversation between them over say a three-month period. The thickness of the lines demonstrates the frequency of verbal exchange. Diagramming a family in this way is not just an empty abstract, academic exercise. It usually reveals hidden patterns, and brings forth new awareness. What do we see in Fig 1? What might we even be able to predict, just from the simple systems diagram?

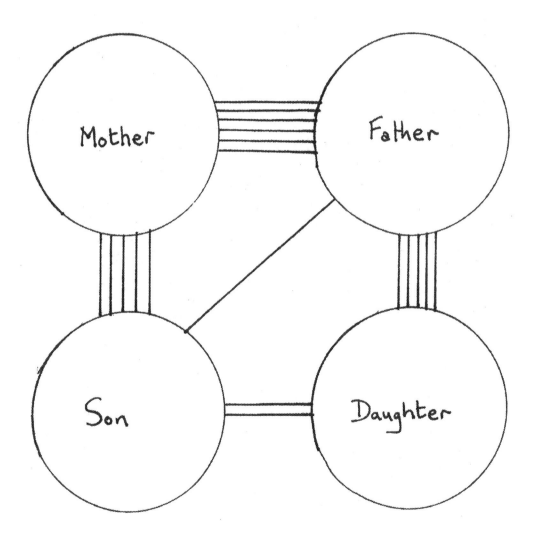

Figure 1: A Family System

We can see that mother and father are strongly inter-connected and that there are strong connections between both parents and the daughter. The son is less connected in this verbal network. He has strong patterns of flow with his mother but fewer with the father and the daughter. He is less integrated into the system. This is an example of the type of awareness that often arises from a diagram of this sort.

We do not stop here, however. We ask more questions of this system. Why does the pattern exist? What historical factors lead it to take this form? What cultural factors might have shaped the system this way? What functions does this arrangement serve? What functions does it seem to prevent from occurring? How does this arrangement affect the family's overall functioning and adaptation to its external environment? What internal dynamics might this arrangement lead to? And so on. One of the beauties of the systems approach is its very capacity to stimulate a series of useful and interesting questions.

To illustrate, we might find that the family we have diagrammed in Fig1 is a "blended family" (very common these days) and that the son in fact is not the biological son of the father. He is the biological son of the mother. The daughter is the biological offspring of both parents in the diagram. The son has significant interactions with his biological father and his father's parents and brothers. In a way Fig 1 is incomplete as a systems diagram, for once these connections across the containing boundary of this nuclear family are entered into the diagram, things become much clearer.

We might expect that the parents of the family diagrammed in Fig 1 (especially the mother) will be striving for a certain degree of what many families seem to desire, a sense of togetherness (often referred to as "cohesiveness"). However, given what we now know, we can predict that this will perhaps be a bit more difficult than is usual owing to the fact that the son (stepson) belongs to two family systems, both of which are quite active and pull on him for membership.

Furthermore, this stepson, insofar as he is a member of both systems—and insofar as he travels from one system to the other (in the form of weekends away, and celebrations enjoyed at one or the other families) is in the vulnerable role of "message carrier" or "boundary person" perhaps even operating as a sort of "gatekeeper" (we will examine these roles in greater depth later in the book). This places him in a vulnerable role. Perhaps some of why this is a vulnerable role is immediately clear to the reader. The dynamics are actually very complex and, again will be dealt with later on. The upshot is that this stepson is more likely to become symptomatic, more likely to become the "identified patient" or the "improper person" than anyone else in the system. Or at least this is what systems theory would predict given this pattern.

Activity 1:
Diagram a family you know about (it could be your family, a family you know, or a family from fiction) using the systems format as in Fig1. Underneath the diagram, write in two awarenesses you gained and two questions that arose from looking at the family from a systems viewpoint.

Awareness/insight
1.

2.

Question
1.

2.

B. Properties of systems

Now that we have defined a system in a broad sense and applied it to families to experience some ways in which systems thinking might help us, we can look at some more specific features of systems and apply yet more of these concepts to families. First...

Systems have boundaries.

The system that we described above has an inside and an outside. There is a boundary demarcating these two areas. Information passes across this boundary from inside the system to the outside and vice-versa. Boundaries are extremely important to systems, much like the skin is important to the human body. If something goes wrong with large areas of our skin, we will have serious problems surviving. This principle applies to systems in general. The management of the boundary is extremely important. Important energy and information comes into the system across the boundary and passes out of the system into the environment. Disruptions in these flows will cause the system to readjust to maintain a balance and in order to survive. Disruptions in the boundary and in boundary functions will also attract a lot of attention and concern, often anxiety, precisely because the boundary is so key in the functioning, definition and survival of the system. We can think of the boundary as a sort of a filter, an energy transmission device and as an early warning mechanism for the system.

If a family is a system then it too will have boundaries that will possess the qualities just mentioned. For example some families will be very private, to themselves, entertain few guests, be "clannish," suspicious of outsiders and reluctant to mix with the surrounding community. Such a family might be said to have somewhat impermeable boundaries. On the other hand there are families with an "open door policy" people seem to join and leave the family frequently, people often live inside the family as a member for extended periods and then leave. This family mixes extensively with its community and you might get the feeling that there is an "Everybody is Welcome" sign over the door. This would be considered a family system with very open boundaries.

Clearly, it will be very different for us if we live in either of these two families. In the first family, we might enjoy the relative orderliness, but miss the frequent contact with the outside world. In the latter, we might enjoy the freewheeling parade of people and experiences, but it might become quite chaotic at times.

Activity 2:
Think of two families you know, one with closed boundaries and one with open boundaries. Write five descriptive sentences for each family in the space below.

1.   **"Open" boundary family.**

2.   **"Closed" boundary family**

What seem to be the consequences of a family having open or closed boundary systems?

Do these families fit the ideas presented on boundaries in this book?

So, boundaries of a family system can be permeable or impermeable. How is this decided? There are many factors that affect boundary permeability of systems, as we shall see—culture plays a role, social class and the members of the system itself play roles in deciding on the permeability of system boundaries. Even technology has an important role. For example, families these days have to decide how much Internet access their children will be able to gain, or what television shows they can view. These are boundary decisions. How they are made will be affected by multiple factors inside the family, notably authority, influence and power. These ideas bring us back to the interrelatedness that we find in systems. Let us make this our second axiom of system functioning...

In a system, everything affects everything else.

Even small alterations in one part of a system can reverberate, often in surprising ways, throughout a system and affect parts of a system that seem a long way away. Sometimes the small initial change gets amplified in a surprising and overwhelming fashion. An adolescent child gets a part time job, gets some extra income, buys a car, gets a new set of friends, has improved self esteem, feels more personal power and pushes for a redefinition of the boundaries around the family. They buy their own computer, want to keep different hours, see a movie at midnight. This leaves the parents at home on their own, with each other with new possibilities for intimacy, if they are ready for it. The younger children who were often in the care of the now mobile adolescent now have to be cared for in another way. Pressure is exerted on the parents. The younger ones even feel a bit neglected and start to let this be known. On and on. Everyday events, rolling through the system in a domino effect. Most of the time participants in families do not anticipate these effects nor do they explain events as perhaps having been brought on by what are many times smaller events at an earlier time. The systems perspective alerts us to the inter-relatedness of things. The saying, "When one family member is sick, the whole family is sick," reflects this style of thinking, and it can be helpful in diagnosing many family situations. If mother gets the flu, we have a "flu-mother-family" or, more seriously, if father gets diabetes mellitus we have a "diabetes mellitus family."

Activity 3:
Describe a sequence of events in a family that illustrates the principle of interconnectedness of systems. Focus your description on an unanticipated outcome resulting from a relatively small initial change in the system.

Let us return to boundaries for a moment, for there is another important axiom of system functioning to explore there.

Boundaries can be lines or regions.

Some systems are surrounded by "lines" such that one is in or out of the system quite quickly, while other systems have "boundary regions," an intermediate zone, where one is neither fully in nor fully outside of the system. For example, some houses have "mud rooms," vestibules, verandahs, patios and so on such that one can visit, be part of the household and yet not be fully inside the house. Other houses (often apartments) have no such intermediate spaces. One is either outside in the hallway or inside in the living room. Usually at the boundaries between countries, there is a boundary region where one is, administratively at least, in between the countries. One does not immediately pass from Italy into Switzerland. There is a gap of some few yards that acts as a buffer zone. For the most part, having a boundary region around a system is functional, so long as the system does not, as a result become too closed or "over bound." The boundary region enables the participants in the system to engage in system transactions reflectively, to examine the types of goods, persons and information that will cross its boundaries and to examine the extent to which that material will or will not assist them in the furtherance of their goals. Systems with thin boundary regions or boundary lines are prone to feeling that decisions regarding the boundary have to be made hastily and unreflectively. This usually increases the level of anxiety in the system and increases the likelihood of impractical decisions being made at the boundary. An application of this axiom can be found if we think of a "blended" family where, say, the daughter spends the weekend with her father, to return on Sunday night to the home of her mother and stepfather. In "systems parlance" she is crossing a boundary from one family system to another. Thinking of this event in this way can alert us to many possibilities. First, crossing boundaries usually stimulates anxiety. Since we are thinking of these as systems, we will assume that everybody is anxious about the return of the daughter. The daughter herself will probably be the most anxious. Another principle of social systems functioning is that the boundary is an anxious place to be, and the daughter is close to and crossing the boundary between these two systems. People handle anxiety in many different ways—fighting, withdrawing, emotional excitation and so on. This anxiety will be maximized if the daughter is not given a sort of "decompression zone" an intermediate time and space for her to drop the culture of the family she has just come from and to adopt the culture and ways of the family she is about to enter.

Another everyday example would be in the way people often need the drive home to exit their work system and prepare to enter their family system. Sometimes even more might be required. In situations of poverty or overcrowding, the maintenance of such boundaries might be seriously compromised, having a deleterious effect on system functioning. Noises from neighboring apartments or the street interfere with system functioning and perhaps cannot be shut out. When one or more of the family have been traumatized, it might be very difficult to shut out the noises from the past, from the unconscious of the family, and system functioning is similarly disrupted.

The next axiom or "rule" of system functioning is...

Systems contain subsystems, which contain...

This axiom of social system functioning alerts us to the way in which systems are nested in a fractal fashion, all intertwined and mutually influencing one another.

Inside the family system are different subsystems. For example, there is the parental subsystem and the children subsystem, and these have a boundary or boundary region between them and there are exchanges across the boundary. Once we have this organizing framework, we can ask some useful questions. For example, "What is the boundary between parents and children like?" Is it very permeable, so that there is little differentiation between parents and children? Is it very impermeable, so that there is little exchange between parents and children? Given that we know what the boundaries are like between the two subsystems, we can go on to ask to what extent the current arrangement meets the family's functional goals. For example, it could be that an impermeable boundary between children and parents is functional in terms of enabling the parents making enough money for the family to survive, but is less than adequate in meeting the children's needs for socialization and attachment, or vice versa. It might be, for example that the parents are very "transparent" and available to the children, but that certain types of dependency needs or needs for privacy in the children are not being met.

Activity 4:
Describe an example of something in a family that shows (a)
impermeable boundaries between parents and children and
(b) permeable boundaries between parents and children.

a.   Permeable Boundaries

b.   Impermeable Boundaries

This next axiom is important in avoiding the negative consequences of "blaming" in social systems....

In systems, causality is distributed.

This principle is often difficult for people to grasp or remember to apply. So much of the way we have been taught and brought up to think about things in modern western society goes against this principle. When we try to explain events, we often look for a cause, or sometimes a set of causes. We seem to have been programmed to think linearly, thus: "A caused B, B caused C and C caused D. Therefore the root cause of the event was A. If we change A in some way we will gain control over D." Clearly the panoply of scientific and technical advances surrounding us demonstrates the utility of this way of thinking. But it is not the only way, and it is not the only useful way. There are numerous other ways of thinking about causality, and systems thinking offers one of them. In systems thinking, for example, causality, instead of being located in one or a few "special" (shall we say, "privileged") places is distributed throughout the system itself, perhaps in something that is uniquely created by the system, something that is thus not an explicit part of the system, perhaps a set of beliefs in the culture, say, of a social system. We can find an example of this when we try to examine, for example, technological accidents, like the two space shuttle disasters. The linear, non-systems view is to locate the problem in a set of "causes," such as failed "O" ring rocket gaskets, or a dislodged wing-tile. On closer, more systemic examination, however, we find that the causes are much more subtle and systems-oriented. There was a set of beliefs in the culture of NASA or of the manufacturers of the shuttle parts, there was the weather, congress, suspicions of kickbacks for sub-optimal designs, public opinion, elections to be won and so on. Now, where is the cause? Of course, the "O" rings did fail, but the "O" Rings themselves were only part of a larger system. If we just replace or improve the "O" rings we have not fully understood the problem, and it will reoccur, only in a different guise, with different details.

It is the same in families. A disaster occurs, say, a husband is discovered having an affair with another woman. Why did this happen? In the non-systemic mode, we seek a causal chain, some of them very simple, such as, "He is a man, and men are like that. The other woman tempted him, and he is weak." A fairly common, conventional explanation. Perhaps we can elongate the causal chain by adding items like, "The wife was perhaps not satisfying him sexually, and his mother was narcissistic and withdrawn, so he was looking for the love he never had as a child." Recall, I am not challenging the veracity of these causal links, merely questioning their usage in a linear fashion. We can jump these linear explanations into systemic ones by noting that many interactions are reciprocal, especially in systems, and immediately the explanatory line becomes a circumplex system. Perhaps the man did have a self-involved mother, and perhaps he selected a sexually withdrawn, cold wife so as to duplicate the relationship he had with his mother. We might find similar reciprocal relations with the wife as the center of inquiry. When we look closely at other factors in the system field the couple was embedded in we also jump up to a systemic approach. Let us say that this couple had two children, a 16-year-old boy and a 19-year-old girl. Both of these children have either left the home (as in the case of the 19-year-old) or are preparing to leave soon (the 16 year old). The parents are finishing up on the major task of bringing up their children in the household. Perhaps they are considering, "What next? What do we do, now that this time and energy-consuming task has been completed? For so long, this was who we were. What are we now?" Perhaps this couple can recover some of the intimacy before the children came. But that might be a challenge. Actually, on deeper inquiry we find that for this couple there was always a child. The older girl was from a previous marriage, and was very young when this couple met. Perhaps this is related to the role she seemed to have as being a vehicle for the tensions between the couple. There were many fights before the 19-year-old left home, especially with the father. Perhaps he was displacing some of his anger and frustration towards his wife onto the oldest daughter. Perhaps her "outsider" role (being "blood related " to another man) set up as the target for his anger. It now becomes interesting that the infidelity occurs a few months after the angry and tumultuous departure of the older child. The man, the couple, the system, perhaps needed another conduit for anger and frustration, but at whom, through whom, with whom? Recall, that in these musings, we are not seeking *the* cause, not even a set of causes. Perhaps we should visualize the causes as occurring in the interactions between these events, in the space between.

Recall too, that none of this means that people can abdicate responsibility, and say, "The system made me do it." Individuals bear, take and live with the responsibility of their actions. Actions are results and causes in a circumplex of multi-layered complex systems. The more we are aware of the operational rules of these systems (and their enormous power) the more responsibility we have, the more responsibility we can take, and (although I hesitate to say this) the more effective our actions will be.

In addition, the conscious choice, by an individual, to change their behavior can have a radical effect on a family system.

Activity 5:

Describe an event of some significance in a family, perhaps one you know (be careful to conceal the identity, by changing names and some details). Perhaps select one from fiction. In section (a) describe the event and its causes in the more usual "linear" way. Using the explanatory structure of "This happened, perhaps it was because of this and that." Then, in section (b) describe it in a more systemic way such that the causal factors are distributed across a large set of factors, perhaps resulting from the systemic interaction of sets of factors in reciprocal relations. Section (a) can be one or two sentences. Section (b) should be at least seven sentences long.

(a)

(b)

Another systemic axiom …..

Systems can be more open or more closed.

When we were discussing boundaries around systems and how these boundaries can be relatively permeable to information or relatively impermeable, the concept of openness and closedness was introduced. It is always like that when one talks of systems. In systems, everything is inter-related and intertwined. Language tends to give us information in a linear fashion so systems are hard to describe or to grasp with language, especially written language (but that is the subject of another book). *A system is said to be open when there is a relatively free and plentiful transfer of information across its boundaries and when the system makes adaptive changes in its internal structure, and in its relation to its environment in response to a significant portion of that information.* An open system is a system that takes in "stuff" from its environment and then changes itself and the way it behaves as a result of the "stuff" it has imported. An open system is therefore a dynamic structure and process, changing in response to changes in its environment. It is not always changing dramatically, for there are times when the environment does not call for a change, but it is ever ready for a change should it receive feedback from the environment that such a change is necessary. Open systems maintain what is known as a **dynamic equilibrium**, *t*hat is, a balance that is forever changing. Open systems, especially the category of open systems called **complex adaptive systems**, which include human social systems, human cognitive and cultural structures and families are in the process of accommodating to and assimilating the environment in which they live, and in the process becoming more and more complex as they become more and more adapted to their environment and to a wider and wider array of niches in their environment.

What does this mean for families? Well, if a family behaved like an open system it would have an active and abundant transfer of energy, information, "stuff" across its boundaries and would demonstrate a readiness to alter its internal structure in the face of telling information that it might take in. For example, a family that was an open system would have a number of contacts in its community, nearby, local, regional, national and global. It would be up-to-date in what is going on in the world from an array of perspectives—social, cultural, aesthetic, emotional, political, religious, technological and so on. Any one of the things on this list can "hit" a family and cause it to change, to adapt. Careers become obsolete as a result of technology, values change as a result of the decline or advance of religious values of different types, families can be sundered by ignorance of health care issues and policies. From this perspective, the managers of a family require all the logistical and strategic planning capacities of managers of companies. In a family that is an open system, people belong to groups outside of the family, take up roles in those groups and bring back information and experiences into the family to enrich it and render it more complex, and thus, more robust in an ever-changing environment. A family that is an open system has an array of social contacts, friends, work-mates and acquaintances from many walks of life. They are not, for example, like the family depicted in the movie,' *"The Garden of the Finzi-Continis"* (by Vittorio de Sica) who live in splendid isolation in their garden, blissfully unaware of the fact that the gathering storm of fascism in Italy is upwelling all around them. The consequences are tragic.

The family that is an open system has a certain unmistakable feel to it. When you enter it, it feels like a buzz of activity, emotional engagement is rife; one feels that the situation is close to "organized chaos," but things seem to work out in the end. It is busy, intense and stuff does seem to get done. There will be conflict. This is inevitable, but the conflict is task-related, that is related to chores that need to get done for the family to function. The conflict is not of the "self sabotaging" type. The open system family is a "going concern."

Can a system be "too open"? Yes. If a family for example has too much of an "open-door" policy, it can become swamped with information flooding in from the environment; too many guests, too many outside commitments, not enough time to maintain internal relationships with one another, or to observe family traditions; all these can overwhelm and disorganize the family. Clearly, as was intimated in the section on boundaries, one of the key tasks of the managers of the family is to regulate the openness of the family—not too open, and (as we shall see in the next section) not too closed.

An open system tends towards self-organization, while a closed system tends towards entropy, or disorganization.

When a system is "open" along the lines we have described, we notice that it tends to organize and re-organize itself around new information that has crossed into its internal workings, constantly updating itself in the face of changing conditions. When a system closes its boundaries, it tends towards a condition known in systems parlance as *entropy,* which means that the system has become disorganized; the system's internal energy is now becoming randomly distributed. A quick way of grasping this would be to imagine an aquarium as a closed system, with no inputs of food, oxygen or fresh water and no outputs of filtration of waste. Pretty soon this closed system aquarium becomes a disorganized mess, populated with slimy blobs—entropy. Families operate according to this systems rule. If the family is too closed, it tends towards entropy, becoming disorganized. If this closed system is opened up to some environmental inputs, then a process of organization will be observed. Again, if a system becomes too open, as noted above, it too will become entropic. We now arrive back at the statements made earlier regarding the importance of the boundary region in the family and of its sensitive management in maintaining family organization.

Activity 6:
Sketch, in a few sentences an example (real or imaginary) of a family that is (a) organized and open and (b) disorganized and closed.

(a)

(b)

Can you think of a family that does not follow these precepts of systems operation? If you can, describe it and state why it seems to operate the way it does.

Open systems have dynamic equilibriums—they exist in a state of ever-changing balance.

A sense of balance is vital in many spheres of activity. Broadly speaking, we can identify three types of balance or equilibrium, (a) *Static equilibrium* that is the balance we have with, say, a slab of rock lying flat on the ground. It is unlikely to tip over. It is not going anywhere, unless considerable force is applied to it. (b) *Unstable equilibrium* that is the balance we have with, say, a house of cards. The balance here is precarious. Even a slight breeze will upset it. Finally, we have (c) *Dynamic equilibrium* that is the type of balance we have in open systems, systems that are constantly readjusting themselves in the face of new feedback from the environment. This is the type of balance we find when we ride a two wheel bicycle. We are balanced, but we are constantly in the process of falling slightly, only to catch ourselves, right ourselves until the next tilt a moment later. Standing up is also an example of dynamic equilibrium, even though it looks like a static equilibrium. When we stand up, we are, usually without our knowing it, constantly adjusting and readjusting our muscle tensions so as to remain erect.

What does this have to do with families? Well from a systems perspective it means a lot. It is also a set of concepts that will give us some important ideas when it comes to managing a family. Many people seem to strive for a stable life. Often this boils down to them seeking a stable equilibrium. A stable equilibrium is found in closed systems. We have already argued that closed systems tend towards entropy, or disorganization. Therefore if we aim for static equilibrium, we end up being disorganized. (Think of how difficult it is to balance on a bike when it is standing still. Once it gets moving and we start seeking a dynamic, instead of a static equilibrium, the task is still tricky, but it is much easier.) We probably need our families, if they are to be functional, to be a relatively open system. This means that we must seek a dynamic equilibrium. The balance that we experience today is qualitatively, quantitatively and experientially different from states of balance that we have had before and that we will have afterwards. This, I believe, is a key point. It means that in order to build and survive in a durable social unit, such as a family, we must be prepared to take the risk of living with the dynamic equilibrium that is part and parcel of an open system. Rather like riding the wave, when we go surfing—exciting but risky. Not all of us are prepared to take risks, and it is usually more difficult to take a risk on our own. And with this last statement, I have introduced the elements of individual personality traits, such as desire for orderliness, predictability and the capacity to bear risk, and psychosocial phenomena such as the presence or absence of support networks or "safety nets" when we "wipe out" or lose our balance. Many cultural assumptions about families purvey the notion that it is possible to achieve a static equilibrium that one can "arrive." If the tenets of systems theory are even partially correct, such cultural assumptions can do harm, and cause much unnecessary suffering.

Activity 7:
Describe a social situation in which you were maintaining a dynamic equilibrium. What were you doing? How did it feel? What were the outcomes? Does your experience jibe with the ideas presented above?

.....another systems axiom.....

Social systems often exhibit a quality that can be called mirroring or simultaneity.

The dynamisms that underlie this phenomenon can be quite complex, and I believe that much yet remains to be understood in this domain. What it refers to is the often noted fact that when a process is operating in one part of a system (say a department of an organization, or the parental subsystem) it will be seen simultaneously, as if it is being mirrored, in another part of the organization (the board of directors of the organization or the children). Often, it is quite difficult to explain how this simultaneity occurs, because the two systems may not have been in contact with one another or they had not been aware of the process occurring in the other subsystem. (For example the board had never met the departmental members and the parental process was, they thought, unknown to the children).

Some of the means whereby such simultaneity can occur in families and other social systems will be explained in the later chapter on the psychodynamic processes that operate in groups and families. For the time being, we can simply be alert to the fact that such processes are likely to occur and, as a result can even help us predict certain family processes.

A prosaic example from my English school days can help illustrate one of the simpler forms of this phenomenon. The teachers were often quite sadistic and often took pleasure in beating the boys. Following this principle, what should we find amongst, say the boys? We lived in a culture saturated in sadism and cruelty. There was an avoidance of tenderness and shows of "weakness" along with a pronounced tendency to pick on the "weak."

A family example might be as follows: a mother has an attitude of contempt for her husband, whom she regards as inept and inadequate. The daughter of the family teases the younger brother until he is virtually paralyzed with anxiety and uncertainty.

Sometimes this precept of simultaneity or mirroring can be seen operating across generations. Qualities that were present in great-great-grandparents can be seen to be lived out by descendants whom they never met. This aspect of this tenet can be beautifully illustrated in the movie "The Joy Luck Club" where, despite the mothers' intense efforts, the daughters still manage to live out life scripts of the ancestors.

This next axiom is not one derived from all systems theory. It is one, however, that I subscribe to very strongly, and that plays a central role in explaining most, if not all, family dynamics.

Human systems have a tendency towards growth, which is here defined as a tendency towards greater degrees of differentiation

and integration. If this tendency is not realized adequately the system will tend towards negative disintegration.

It is as if the human being comes equipped with a very core line of "programming" that states, "You must grow." It would make sense for a complex adaptive organism like the human being to have such a pre-programming because it is essential that its internal representations of the world are "kept up to date," not only with changes and vicissitudes in the physical environment but also with developments in the social and cultural fields. When this program in the human being is not adequately fulfilled, alarm systems are set off to alert the organism and the social system that something needs to be done to update its internal images. Often these alarm systems take the form of "symptoms," for example, depression, anxiety or various other types of "acting out." The human being and the social systems it forms are learning systems, gathering information, storing it, re-organizing, re-combining information in novel ways, perhaps more compressed and economical ways so as to better its adaptation.

Applying this to families yields some interesting viewpoints. The family, then, is a learning organism, gathering information and re-combining it so that it is better adapted to its environment. If it does not adequately update its programs, then symptoms will appear, not only because the family is less well adapted to its environment, but also from the very basic concern that arises when a complex adaptive system is not learning enough. This will set off alarm buttons in the system to the effect that a very basic program is being violated, just as an alarm is activated when we are not breathing enough oxygen.

On a more practical level, we can ask of the family, "What is being learned? What new information have we gathered? How have we recombined old information we have had for a while?" A practical example is fairly easy to find. Families have to constantly learn new things about their members and the outside world. What new things did my child learn this week? What are my partner's sexual likes and dislikes? What does the future look like economically? How did I feel when I was sixteen? The list is endless.

An open, growing family system seems to be driven a lot by inherent human curiosity and is affected by all the anxieties and concerns that attend curiosity. "Curiosity killed the cat." Lot's wife was turned to stone perhaps because of her curiosity. A child's asking, "Where do babies come from?" or, ""Mommy, why are you crying?" can stimulate anxiety. Sometimes so much anxiety is stimulated that curiosity is stunted and the system starts to slow down in its rate of learning—the "You must re-program" code is violated and even more anxiety is created. The family starts to become seriously "symptomatic." Perhaps a key is the re-stimulation of curiosity and learning, the provision of support to help bear the anxiety of learning so that the system can get back on track, as an open, adaptive system.

Growth in systems can sometimes be smooth and continuous and sometimes can take the form of "positive disintegration."

Much of the time we are growing and we do not even realize it. We can learn new skills, develop new competencies, gain new insights in a small-scale incremental way and only realize how much we have changed after a while, perhaps when we meet a friend we have not seen for a couple of years and they say, "My, you have changed!" This is a pleasant comfortable way of growing, rather like setting a nice comfortable pace and incline on a treadmill.

Other times growth is much more like a "positive catastrophe." It can be very disruptive when the old ways just will not work any more, and a sort of revolution takes place in the self. Common examples would include the "midlife crisis" or some adolescence. The system goes through, what is called, in systems parlance, a **step function**. All the settings on the system are changed and the system starts to operate very differently. Of course, humans will still breathe oxygen, but significant features change radically. We are different after puberty and the attendant growth spurt. A couple is very different after the birth of its first baby. A couple is different after the children leave home. The death of a parent, the loss of a cherished job, all of these can act as *culminating events* that trigger a radical change in the individual or the system—a step function. It is rather similar to how one last flake of snow creates the avalanche, or one more drip of water bursts the dam. Something gives way; there is temporary chaos and then re-organization, with a new arrangement.

Not all disintegration therefore is negative. It may all feel negative, and at times very inconvenient, and all disintegration may place the individual in a very vulnerable situation (just as lobsters and hermit crabs are vulnerable when they change shells) but some disintegration is positive insofar as it signifies an opportunity for the emergence of a more complex, better adapted organization. Sometimes children seem to go to pieces around puberty and adults too at midlife, yet somehow, they come out the other side, we hope, much more expansive and integrated individuals. Sometimes, too, families seem to come out the other end of a chaotic crisis stronger, more resilient and durable.

How can one tell the difference? For if there are these two forms of disintegration, it would be very useful to be able to tell when one is going to pieces in a constructive versus a destructive way. This is complex, of course, but one way is to look at the whole person, family or individual and ask, "Is the whole system regressing (going backwards) or is there, on balance more forward movement than backward. If, on an overall basis, the person or the family is moving forward (i.e. learning and growing) even though there are significant areas of regression or chaos, then the disintegration is probably of a positive kind. If, however, there are relatively few areas of forward movement, then the disintegration is of a negative nature. Thus, for example, a pubertal child starts to act up and act in a very infantile way, but they still have good friends, show up to school, keep reasonable grades, then the child is probably disintegrating in a positive way. This does not mean we just ignore them, and say "They are just going through a stage" It means that the need for support and concern is still there, but not in the same form and extent as for a child who is disorganized in a more global fashion.

Activity 8:
Describe a family that you have observed go through the process of learning something. What was learned? How was it learned? Were there stages in the learning process—a beginning, middle, and an end?

C. Eight aspects of social systems

Whenever I have to think about a social system, such as a family, and attempt to make some sense of it, I find it can be helpful to go through the following checklist of the eight domains of social systems. For each of these domains, I attempt to generate some sentences on the properties of the social system I am dealing with. This has the effect of uncovering many aspects of systems functioning that might otherwise remain hidden. By going through all of the eight domains, I can be sure that I am taking multiple perspectives. This not only ensures that I am getting good coverage of the system I am trying to understand, it also can stimulate my creativity.

Social systems can be "diagnosed" by examining their properties in eight domains:

FANTASIES
PHANTASIES
FEELINGS
BOUNDARIES
AUTHORITY
ROLES
TASKS
RULES

We can thus more fully "grasp" a family system if we ask, "What is going on?" in each of these domains. What might this involve?

Fantasies are the imaginary aspects of family life. They can be positively or negatively toned, relatively in touch or relatively out of touch with reality. Examples of fantasies might be, "We never get mad at each other." Or "My mother is perfect." Or "I am the black sheep of the family" or "He is exactly like his father." Fantasies might also take the form of **family myths—** shared fantasies, such as, "We Smiths are the most special family in the neighborhood." Or "We Zokowskis always stick together." Fantasies serve many functions in families, they can create cohesion, magnify rifts, uplift hope, create despair. They are often organized around episodes or narratives that are shared, sometimes recurrently at family get-togethers, as if to solidify their reality, or as if to get a "buy-in" from key family members.

Phantasies are exactly the same as fantasies except that they are unconscious. These are the imaginary elaborations in the family that are not as available in the discourse of the family. They lie beneath the surface. They will show up in the dreams of individuals in the family, in repeated patterns of behavior of the family as a whole, in inter-generational patterns, in repeated symptoms in the family. If these unconscious phantasies are brought to the surface, there is usually a good deal of anxiety in the family; that after all is why they are kept "in the basement," because they are anxiety-provoking. There is often a solid resistance in the family against uncovering phantasies—it is as if it would break the rules, roles and the prevailing system of authority in the family, or any other social system, for that matter. The phantasies are closely allied to the notion of **family secrets**—"secrets," like "Grandfather was in the SS.," or "Aunt Hattie worked in a bordello"—which when spoken about are often found to be common knowledge and a secret at the same time. These phantasies are kept in the unconscious by a lattice of unconscious collusive agreements and alliances the exact nature of which we shall examine later. They can play an enormously important role in maintaining the status quo in families.

Feelings refers to the emotions, moods and passions that typify the family. Is this a family that, for example, makes emotional contact through anger or joy? What are the rules governing feelings in the family? Are there rules against certain feelings, such as sadness, regret, anger or pride? How are these rules regarding feelings enforced? What is the prevailing **mood** in the family? Is it "down" or "up"? Is it low-key or edgy? How does the mood set the tone for the emergence of certain types of feelings, which are typically shorter-lived than a mood, which can go on for a long time? If there is a prevailing mood of irritability in the system then the emotions or passions of tenderness might be harder to take hold. What are the underlying rationalizations for the spectrum of feelings one finds in the family? Is there an assumption that certain types of feelings are *déclassé?* Are certain feelings regarded as being signs of weakness or mental illness? Are certain emotions likely to cost one a sense of authority? Feelings are often driven by assumptions and sometimes the assumptions are more in the nature of fantasies or phantasies.

Boundaries have been discussed earlier in one of their forms. In this context, they can also refer to the very categories that the family has evolved, the edges it has established between, say reality and fantasy, the differentiation of the roles taken up by family members and the sense of individuality that is permissible in the family. Are members of the family felt to be "independent operators" or are they seen as fused with the rest of the family, so that actions are checked back with the entire group before being embarked upon? How are the issues of privacy dealt with in the family? How are tensions around private and public information managed?

Authority has to do with the deployment of power within the family. Who has power over what, and how is that power maintained and manifested? What are the symbols of power in the family? Is authority reflected in seating arrangements, in patterns of conversation, in physical contact, in eye contact? Who are the leaders? Who are the followers? How do family members feel about this arrangement of leadership and followership? Is there a leadership vacuum? Why? Are there efforts at re-arranging patterns of authority, re-arranging the way decisions get made in the family? Does this show up in competition? If so, how is this managed? Is it out in the open or surreptitious, sabotaging competition. How do experiences with leadership, power and authority early in the lives of family members affect the use and deployment of power and authority in the present?

Are there domains, in which certain individuals in the family have greater power? For example, does the mother make decisions regarding finance, loans, bills, credit and so on, while the father has authority in areas to do with the bigger disciplinary issues? Does this distribution of power jibe well with personal preferences and other aims?

Individuals in the family will also have different assumptions regarding authority. For example, many parents believe that they derive "position power" simply from being in the role of mother or father. Other parents might feel that power is something that has to be earned and maintained through behaviors that cause others to respect and admire them. Yet others may believe that providing for material well-being creates power—they may believe that they gain and maintain power over the family by being a good provider. Similarly assumptions regarding power will vary among the children. Not infrequently members of the same family will have different assumptions regarding power and its deployment and this can create conflicts. A mother who believes that she has position power by virtue of being "the mother" may well ask the father, who believes that the respect that comes with authority is to be in large part, earned, "Are you going to let them talk to me that way?" when the child questions a decision. Similarly, this couple may have different assumptions about arguing in front of the children. Some parents will believe that open arguing weakens their power as a united front, while others may feel that such transparency in the leadership actually aids in the consolidation of their power.

Parents, the managers of the family system will also vary in the extent to which they believe power and authority should be distributed among family members. For example, they may disagree on the timetable they have as to when a child is able to become an independent operator in a given domain. In the culture of the United States, for example there are a number of markers throughout adolescence that empower the adolescent, almost by degrees—a driver's license, the right to earn money, the right to open a line of credit, the right to vote, the right to drink alcoholic beverages. Similarly the responsibilities society expects the adolescent to shoulder increase, for example, he might be charged as an adult for a crime, or asked to serve in an armed conflict. As this transition, which can take several years, takes place, so the distribution of power shifts in the family, creating new alliances, creating new conflicts, surfacing old anxieties and depressions. The politics of the family are often turbulent during this era. Of course, the drive towards independence has been operating since birth, thus power has always been part of family life. During middle and late adolescence, however, the stakes seem higher.

When one looks at the family this way, it is almost as if it is a business, with departments, that can work in greater or lesser co-ordination around their various tasks. Many families have tensions along these basic lines.

Roles, if we are to fully grasp the dynamics of a family, are extremely important. They are also extremely complex, with multiple layers, crosscuts and tensions. Let us step in to this tangled web.

First, roles can be **formal** or **informal.** The **formal** roles are reasonably easy to ascertain, they include things like "father," "son," "stepmother" and so on. These are the culturally driven and culturally given labels that we give to family members. But very soon, the simplicity fades and we encounter complexity. First, different cultures have different expectations regarding the fulfillment of various roles. These expectations can also change through time. The culture of motherhood was very different for my mother in 1955 than it is for a mother in 2007. We will examine these cultural factors in a later chapter. Secondly, individuals will vary in the way in which they receive these cultural messages. Culture is not a one-way street. Certainly, the individual gets messages from the culture as to how they should be a "good father" or "brother," but many, perhaps all, individuals take these expectations and creatively shape them to their own will and preferences. Some individuals actively seek to change the cultural expectations regarding family roles. Thirdly, many family roles, although they are labeled clearly, do not carry clear expectations regarding role performance. For example, the role of "stepfather" is probably increasing in frequency in the United States, but, as yet, it seems the formal definition of the role and its expectations for a good performance are lacking. Finally, as families alter in form with increasing rapidity in the postmodern era, there are roles for which the culture has not even yet developed a label, and it would seem highly unlikely that a clear set of role expectations can exist for a role for which no label, as yet, exists. For example, in the United States, there is no label for, "the children of my wife's ex husband's second wife" or, "the children of my wife's uncle's second wife" or "the daughter of my wife's closest friend who is living with me and calls me 'uncle'." The reader can probably come up with several of these from his or her own experience.

An additional complexity I have observed in this realm results from the high frequency of long distance migrations in the modern era. Sometimes, parents residing in a poorer nation or region will migrate to a richer nation seeking economic advantage. A young child might be left behind in the care of a grandparent or other relative, so that the parents are left free of childcare responsibilities to build a new life in the new country. In the meantime the grandparent, or another relative, fulfills the role of parent and the child bonds to them, especially if the child is very young. Several years later the child is brought to reunite with the parents, who frequently expect the child to recognize the blood relatedness of the close "blood relationship." However, the child will often be traumatized by the separation from the relative with whom they have bonded, and, if the separation has been protracted enough, will see the parents as strangers with whom they have to bond all over again. I have worked with several individuals with this or a similar history in my private practice. They are suffering from (at least) three layers of compounded trauma. One, there was the initial separation from the parents when they migrated. Two, there was the second separation from the care taking relative. Three, there was the denial of there being any loss in either case. These individuals thus frequently underestimated the intensity of the strain they had been under in childhood. They typically had disturbed love relationships in adulthood, for these, as we shall see in an upcoming chapter, are intimately tied up with the nature of the early childhood attachments. The point being made in this section, however, is that simply because one has a label on one's role in a family, a label such as "mother" or "father," one cannot safely assume that one actually performed that role. In the examples just cited, the parents had the labels of "mother" and "father," but did not carry all the emotional baggage of those terms—this probably belongs to the long lost grandmother, back in the old country.

A similar interesting dynamic sometimes occurs in the homes of the wealthy, when a child might bond more thoroughly and completely with a nurse, nanny or servant than with, say a rather cool and distant parent. Again, the nanny might be fired or the family may move on and the child suffers extreme anguish, because they looked upon the nanny as fulfilling the role of "mother"—now an empty space in the child's life. Many parents, who like to think that because they have the role label of "parent" will all too easily overlook and deny this pain in the child, for to do so would be to admit that the child loved the "help" more than them. Again, in adulthood, these "love triangles," "bifurcations in love" and love across class barriers will be repeated, often hidden behind a veil of mystery.

Activity 9:
Think of a family relationship that you have experience of that has no culturally given label for the roles involved. Describe this relationship and comment on the emotional tone of the participants in this relationship. What ideas emerge from you observation?

Further complications arise, but further insights also, if we move on to the concepts surrounding **role tension.** People, family members, can feel all kinds of tensions; one cluster of them has to do with role tension. There are different types of role tension. One is role conflict. There are several types of role conflict. One is when one's personality is in conflict with the role (formal or informal) one is called upon to perform. For example, a teenage boy, often enough concerned with exploring his identity and consolidating some career choices, while differentiating himself from the matrix of his family of origin, will quite possibly feel in personal conflict with the behaviors expected of the role "father," yet he may be called upon to do this should the actual father die. The inverse might be said of a "perpetual adolescent" 45-year-old man. Perhaps here, the boy was encouraged not to move into role performances of a father-type, perhaps because his family of origin, for various reasons found this anxiety producing. A 12-year-old girl may be unready to let go of the role of "child" and take up the role of "teenage child," perhaps because traumatic experiences robbed her of a good deal of her childhood. Thus, when she starts to menstruate, it stimulates profound feelings of loss, sadness and rage in her—feelings that are usually hard to cope with and result, perhaps, in her becoming more "difficult."

Very frequently individuals in families experience **role overload and multiple role conflict.** These occur when an individual is asked to perform two or more conflicting roles. This will result in the familiar feeling of "having to be something different for everybody." Single parents frequently suffer from this. They will often have to perform the role of breadwinner, which takes them away from the children, and parent, which requires extended contact with the children. Or they may feel that they have to perform the role of nurturer and be soft and available, and coach and disciplinarian which involves firmness and distance. Or we may have an aging parent in the house who wants us to let them be independent, but who tends to leave the gas on or fall over if left alone too long. Many roles have to be filled if the family is to be a going concern, and it is extremely difficult to arrange for the performance of these roles in an effective way. Bear in mind, too, that the system is dynamic. The roles of last year will not work today. Roles are shifting as new tasks emerge in the family or as new people arrive and leave.

Each one of these aspects of social systems interacts with all the others. Thus, for example, "roles" interacts with "authority." One might for example have a formal role to fulfill, but for various reasons not have enough authority to carry the role out to the full. One might, for example, have the formal, traditionally-defined role of "father," and wish to carry out that role, but for reasons of say, unemployability, or lack of certain competencies, be unready to fulfill that role. This can generate serious tensions in the family and in the individual. Sometimes social systems (and this still includes families) will seem to unconsciously elect people into roles they are not ready for so as to sabotage the performance of certain functions in the family. The easiest examples to help grasp this phenomenon come from industry and the military. For example, a department may consciously choose an incompetent leader who will be under-authorized so as to avoid having to perform certain unpleasant functions, or they may select someone for a leadership position who will "go easy on them" as a means of expressing their dislike for the organization of which they form a part. In a similar way, a family may unconsciously ask an individual who is clearly unsuited for a role to perform that role so as to sabotage certain functions, which, if performed, would stimulate intense anxiety. Thus, a family, that has a great deal of anxiety around discipline, may insist that the easy-going father, who is a pushover, be the one who is primarily responsible for disciplinary action, thus ensuring that the family stays in a less-than-organized state. These covert processes are subtle, and difficult to grasp. A later chapter will examine them in depth. For the time being, let us note that there are **conscious explicit roles** and **unconscious implicit and covert roles.** One might, for example have the role of "mother" consciously and explicitly, while unconsciously one also carries another role, say, that of "the one who has all the strong feelings." Or, one might have the conscious explicit role of "oldest son," while the covert role is that of "bad seed." It is as if the family is comprised of multiple shifting layers of roles—roles that interact with each other, sometimes harmoniously, but much of the time with a great deal of tension—tension not only between roles occupied by different people, but also tensions between roles carrying different demands within the same person. The situation is indeed complex.

It is also important to ask how flexible the family is in terms of its capacity to shift roles, especially in the face of a changing internal and external family environment. Sometimes families' roles become extremely compacted and stuck and the family has difficulty adapting to a new situation, as might occur when someone leaves home, gets sick or gets promoted. In other families the roles might be extremely fluid and undefined, rather like playing on a sports team where people do not play in their position, and little gets done; people become very frustrated. Structural family therapists will frequently focus on this dynamic, observing, for example, how fixed the family might be in its seating arrangement (the seats usually corresponding to a role) and observing what happens in the family dynamics as the therapist asks members to sit in different seats.

Here are some more classic informal, covert and usually unconscious roles taken up in families:

Placator: I will make sure no-one fights.
Rescuer: If you get into trouble, I will be there.
Whipping boy/girl: If there is a problem, blame me.
Wet blanket: If you having too much fun, I will change that.

Gatekeeper: I will decide what's in and out of bounds.
Policeperson: I will make sure you keep the rules.
Addict: I will act out all the impulses.
Eternal child: I will never grow up for you.
Nurse: If you have an"owie," come to me!
Hypochondriac: I will always be sick for you.
Mediator: I will act as the go-between and message carrier.
Moderator: I will absorb the intense feelings and calm them.
Kidney: I will absorb and purify the poison in the family.
Nun/Priest: I will redeem the family.
Golden boy/girl: I will succeed for you all.
Visionary/psychotic: I will contain all the family's wild thoughts.

The list can be very, very long. It is very important to remember that these roles are not simply taken up by the individuals concerned. The entire family has, as it were, unconsciously selected individuals to play these roles for an array of reasons. Usually the reasons involve protecting the family from undue anxiety. For example, a family may have the belief that it suffers from intense guilt owing to some deeds committed in reality or in fantasy in the past. There may also be a good deal of cultural and religious emphasis on guilt that affects this family. The family then might be very prone to select from among its members an individual to perform the role of nun or priest, who could act as an offering of expiation to some church, and thus cleanse the family of its sin. Of course, sometimes the individual is ideally suited for the role, but very often, this is not the case and many intrapsychic and interpersonal tensions arise.

Activity 10:
Think of a family with which you are familiar. First list the formal roles for this family. Next list the covert roles often performed by the family members. Finally, comment on two tensions that you identify in the family that result from the roles you observe.

FAMILY MEMBERS   **FORMAL ROLES**   **COVERT ROLES**

TENSION 1:

TENSION 2:

"Pets and Mascots": Pets can play very important roles in families. I have worked with families where the dog, as far as the children were concerned, was the sanest member. It was the dog that best played the role of "emotional safe haven" or "consistent companion." These assertions do not seem so ludicrous if we recall that in systems, very small components can have dramatic effects—a wing tile, or an "o" ring is a very small part of a shuttle system, but when it fails, the results are disastrous. Furthermore, to pursue the analogy, the wing tile or "o" ring design and maintenance on the shuttle is an expression of the system's culture. Similarly for pets—they can play crucial roles in the maintenance of the family's psychodynamic equilibrium and they express key elements in the family's culture. Pets, for example can also serve as scapegoats for the family, being punished for crimes and misdemeanors that truly belong elsewhere. Pets might be the only living thing in the family that it is safe to hug or snuggle. I have seen pets serve as representations of parts of family members' personalities. Thus, a dog might be treated as if it were a starving victimized tramp, the dog standing for a part of a key family members personality that feels as though it is a starving victimized tramp. It is felt that it is safer to have this part of the personality take up residence in the dog rather than to have a human being live it out. I once knew a boy whose mother had thrown his cat out of a 19th floor window. In a very serious way, the mother and the boy were still falling.

Pets can come and go quickly in families. These passings are significant for one who would wish to understand family life, but are often skated over by families.

Activity 11:
Think of a family that has at least one pet. What role do you think the pet plays for the family? How does the family involve the pet in its imaginary life? What fantasies and stories are told about the pet? What are the themes of these stories? Do they relate in any way to themes that are active in the rest of this family's life? What issues might this family have to face if the pet was not there? What insights did you gain from thinking about this family's pet?

Tasks: Systems are organized around tasks, and work is done in systems towards those aims or ends. There are a number of important crosscutting concepts in this domain. First is the notion of the **primary task**. The primary task (or tasks) is the task or set of tasks that have to be performed if the system is to survive. If these tasks are not performed, then the system will become disorganized and cease to exist. Many times, there might be a lag time between the cessation of the meeting of the primary task and the death of the system, since systems will often have reserve supplies of energy or may be able to survive at a reduced level of functioning for a while before death occurs. For example, a primary task of the family might be the generation of wealth or purchasing power. (I state it in this abstract fashion deliberately, because not all families use money all the time, many, for example barter, or exchange labor, and this must be taken into account.) If the family ceases to perform this function, it may be able to survive for a while, but, unless there are considerable savings or other assets that can be liquidated (like the sale of land or a house or cattle) the family will soon be at risk of breaking up— children being sent to other families or institutions or perhaps the parents breaking up.

Secondary tasks are tasks that support the primary tasks or are adventitious, ancillary functions. For example, laundering one's clothes is not a primary task (for most of us), but helps increase the effectiveness of the performance, perhaps of the primary task of generating income.

These two sets (primary tasks and secondary tasks) are not, however, clear-cut, especially in families, and this adds greatly to the complexity of family life. In a business that is making nuts and bolts, for example, the primary task is fairly easy to identify, as are the secondary tasks. *But what is the primary task of a family? What are families **for?***

Activity 12:
With a group of people, list the primary tasks of families.
What functions does a family serve?

1. _____
2. _____
3. _____
4. _____
5. _____
6. _____
7. _____
8. _____
9. _____
10. _____
11. _____
12. _____
13. _____
14. _____

Others:

Look at your list. Write an awareness you have in reflecting upon this list.

Following is a list of tasks for families culled from the literature on families. Compare it to the list you just developed.

Tasks of Families

Economic security
    Socialization
        Sex
            Reality testing
                Attachment
                    Emotional support
                        Stability
                            Meaning-purpose
                                Growth

Now let us look at what each of these means.

Economic security—Families serve the function of creating an economic safety net for their members. Families generate income and provide backup, at times, for individuals when they fall on hard times. Families also provide members with capital that might be needed in a new economic venture, such as financing school, or a small business loan. Family also provides means of organizing property, for example, through inheritance practices and property rights.

Socialization—Families are used to "bring up children," and this is what is meant by socialization here (It is in the sense that is used by sociologists). It is through families that individuals are taught the values, mores and beliefs of their cultures. The parents act as interpreters and transmitters of their understanding of the culture. In this they instill a social sense with all its appurtenances; social concern, or the lack of it, guilt, shame, or their lack and a complex array of attitudes, values, expectations and beliefs. True, in the modern era, other agencies have been enlisted into this function—schools, media such as TV, video games and compact discs—but much has occurred in the family in the way of socialization in, say, the first three to five years of life before the child can decode these media in any extensive or prolonged manner, so the influence of family in socialization is still of the utmost power, especially if one believes, as I do, in the extreme potency of early childhood experiences in the formation of deep and enduring personality features. Frequently, simply being part of a family provides a vehicle for achieving a sense of conformity and of gaining access to other means of socialization such as school, rituals and pastimes.

Sex—Families serve to regulate sexuality in society. They do this first through socialization, education of the children regarding attitudes towards sexuality and through expectations regarding sexuality and marriage. Marriage and its associated assumptions regarding fidelity, adultery, "cheating" and availability for sexual relationships serves to channel and harness sexual energy in a society, by setting up powerful "rules" regarding who can have sex with whom and under what conditions. This seems to serve the function of a social organizer, adding a certain degree of predictability and regularity to social, sexual and economic life. Economic life is regulated by this regulation of sexuality since marriage and sex serve to define rules of inheritance and rights to property.

Reality testing—Families are very important in the way in which individuals discriminate between reality and fantasy. This overlaps with "socialization" above. In fact, all of these tasks overlap with one another. We can see it occurring, for example when a parent attempts to convince a child that there "is not a monster under the bed" or that "of course Santa Claus is real," and helps at demarcating reality from the imaginary. Or we might see it in the way a parent decides when and how to talk to their child about "the facts of life" and just how "real" this discourse might be. We might also see this in a parent talking to an adolescent about her fantasies of being a "hip hop artist" or of playing for a team in the English Premier League. How much should we support their dreams or bring them down to earth? Adults reality test too. In fact human beings, I believe, are constantly reality testing, trying to achieve **consensual validation** and the sense of security that derives from it. We seem to get very anxious when our take on reality is radically at odds with those around us. For example, a woman might come home and ask their partner, "I had this argument today at work. I think I responded the right way. What do you think?" Or, going home from a party a couple might check out their impressions of the other couples they met, as if to do a "reality check." Not to be part of a family or a group that serves as a surrogate for a family places a stress on the individual in terms of their daily need to reality test, and this can be quite disorienting.

Attachment—Human beings, especially when they are young, have a very strong need for attachment, attachment to selected individuals, and attachment to a group, especially a small group. When this deep need for attachment is met, the individual feels a sense of security, a security that releases them to explore and learn. When these deep needs for attachment security are not met, the individual's energies become diverted towards anxious maneuvers aimed at securing attachment with significant others or at energy-consuming maneuvers aimed at reducing the experienced need for attachment, such as withdrawal or indifference. Families can be excellent formats for meeting this human (primate, in fact) need for secure attachment. Unfortunately, much of the time, events occur that disrupt the family in the performance of this task, usually with very serious social costs. It is this task of the family, the task of meeting the need for reliable human attachment, that illustrates well how the many tasks that families face can often conflict with one another. For example, a family, in order to achieve economic security (and

40

this is especially true of industrial and post-industrial societies) may have to spend long periods of time at a distant workplace, away from their children, who have their needs for ongoing reliable attachment with a relatively small set of others, thwarted. This may also occur when families are required, for economic reasons to uproot and relocate.

Families are enormously complex. Important aspects of this complexity are a) that the family has so many primary tasks, and b) that these tasks are often in conflict with one another. The managers of families (the parents) are therefore frequently faced with complex and difficult problems, problems that have not optimal, but only satisfactory solutions. This situation stands in stark counterpoint to strong elements of popular culture that purvey the notion of simple, problem free, "happy" families. In so doing, it is my belief that great harm is done, for it engenders widespread notions among those who are struggling with the real problems that real families face, a sense of failure and inferiority, which is in and of itself extremely debilitating and counterproductive.

Attachment needs are consistently under played in much of modern "western civilization." John Bowlby and Mary Ainsworth, who were the pioneers of attachment research, faced much opposition to their ideas. Only after a long fight were changes made, for example, in letting parents stay overnight with their young children during hospital stays. There is still a long way to go. Much psychopathology is caused, in the opinion of this author, by ignoring the powerful human need for a secure attachment. The so-called "war on drugs" is being fought in the streets of cities, in ports and in the coca fields of Latin America. The front might be better conceived as existing in cribs and playrooms and in families. I hypothesize that a child with a secure attachment, rarely grows up to be an adult or adolescent that is in need of drugs. When the need for attachment is not adequately met, the individual is prone to overwhelming experiences of emptiness and consequent meaninglessness. (This is a topic of another book of mine.) If these experiences are too profound, and there is not enough emotional support, many troublesome "symptoms," such as the heavy use of intoxicants or "acting out" is very likely, since the individual may be unable to creatively convert the emptiness into a new and deeper meaning system.

Emotional support—This task of families is close to the task of attachment. In fact, attachment is an element of this subset. But attachment is so important in my opinion; it deserves its own category.

We frequently turn to our family when we need emotional support. They may be very good or not so good at offering support, but these are the people to whom we turn when we are weak, vulnerable or upset. We fail a driving test. We get a positive result on a medical test. We lose a job. We get in a fight. We get upset and we are very likely to turn to our family. They may listen, advise, berate us or give us a hug, but on balance, having a family can and often is an important moderator of stress. This has enormous impacts on our psychological well being as well as our physical welfare. Families may give us problems that raise our blood pressure, but they also can offer the support and "containment" that help us relax, calm ourselves, feel confident and regain a low blood pressure. In this way, a good family life *can* extend our lives.

Emotional support is not all hugs and kisses. Many times support can come in the form of vigorous confrontive coaching; as when a parent or sister or wife might tell you that it is time to take some action, or that you are not doing the "right thing." This too is support insofar as it can guide and instill confidence or help one to "snap out of it," and gain some confidence in facing a challenge.

Stability—Families can provide a sense of emotional security, strong feelings of attachment and economic security, but, since there is often a routinized way in which these tasks are carried out, and since there is a formal and informal agreement to continue to perform these tasks within a family (for example, there are legally binding marriages and cultural forces aimed at sustaining intra familial cohesion), individuals operating within a reasonably functional family can plan on certain tasks being fulfilled in the short and medium term. This not only provides emotional and social security, it has the effect of freeing up energy in the family that can be aimed at other objectives—objectives that go beyond survival. In this way, a family can act as a good springboard for its members. For example, an individual who feels relatively secure that their basic financial and emotional needs will be met can broaden their horizons, plan for the future and take some chances—they can go to graduate school, start up a small business, give some presentations, and stretch their scope of activities at work. They might feel that they can take these chances, because there is a secure base at home from which they are operating. An artist or a creative scientist might be more willing, for example, to create a new and unorthodox theory or object if they know there is backing at home. Stability is as important a need in humans as the need to explore. Balancing this dynamic equilibrium is a major ongoing challenge for individuals and groups.

Meaning-Purpose—Human beings can endure enormous hardships and exert exceptional efforts over extended periods of time if they are sustained by a sense of purpose, if their efforts have meaning to them. Take away the sense of meaning and very soon the effort makes no sense and they become demoralized, reduce their efforts and quit. If there is nothing new for them that has a sense of meaning then humans are very prone to the experience of emptiness. I have written at length on this experience in another book, "The Experience of Emptiness." People derive meaning in their lives from many sources. For some it is in religion, or money. For others it might be in gaining power and prestige. For yet others, it might be in helping others or gaining insight into nature's ways. There are many ways of organizing the sense of purpose and meaning in one's life. However, for many people, the core meaning in their life revolves around their family; however it might be defined for them. Thus, we might argue that a primary task of the family is to provide people with a sense of purpose in life. The family we live in helps life and its vicissitudes (its ups and downs, twists and turns) make sense. It is all aimed at something. For many people, that something lies in the fulfillment of their dreams for their family. Thus, take away the family and many people are cut adrift from a deeply felt sense of purpose and they float, aimless and empty. Now this is extremely interesting, because some cultures and some productive systems are very supportive of ongoing family life, while others (that are often very materially efficient) make maintaining a sustained family very difficult. In these latter cultures and productive systems, we would therefore expect to find larger numbers of people cut adrift from the meaning and purpose that is provided for in a very available way by participation in a family group. An example of a "family unfriendly" culture would have to be one that is typical of unregulated industrialized capitalism where market forces and rapid technological development reduce family cohesion and routinely requires that family members relocate. Another example of a family unfriendly culture would be a totalitarian state where allegiance to the family is seen as hostile to loyalty to the state or "the people" and family bonds are thus de-emphasized. In this latter case an alternative meaning system may be provided for in the form of a state or religious ideology, and this may buffer the sense of meaninglessness. In the former case, it is frequently left up to the individual to synthesize his or her own meaning system using their own resources or to adopt the pursuit of wealth itself as a meaning. It appears that, given current conditions, many individuals are not capable of doing this, and have to turn to "social prosthetics" (such as cults, and fanatical groups) or painkillers (such as drugs and other numbing devices and procedures) as a way of getting by.

Many people find their families very interesting and meaningful. They are a "project" that engages their energies. Often times they are a project that "keeps you going" for decades. When the family project changes in form, when, say, children grow up and leave home, the project must be reconstructed. Again this can be a difficult period, a period when the guts of one's sense of what life is all about have been torn out. As Gramsci states, (in his "Prison Notebooks") "The old has died and the new has not yet been born, and in the interregnum, all sorts of morbid symptoms occur."

Growth: Psychosocial Development—As previously asserted, human systems come with a "growth imperative"—an internal code that demands that the system increase in complexity—differentiation and integration of functions. Elsewhere this might be called a "self actualizing tendency" or the tendency to become a "fully functioning person." It is as if human beings have an inbuilt code with an attendant developmental set of phases, or stages, that, on some level, in some way, must be lived through. In other literature these stages might be called "developmental tasks." We each have a developmental task—a project that might take from several months to several decades to realize. We work on these developmental tasks in families. In fact, I would assert that, *the family is **the** social unit in which people work on, realize and achieve their life tasks and which supports them (we hope) in achieving their life task.*

What is a life task? In abstract language, a life task *is a psychosocial challenge face by an individual, the accomplishment of which enhances their functioning, helps in achieving subsequent stages and life tasks and which is a benefit to the social group of which the individual is part.*

In more concrete language, it might involve an individual developing a capacity to trust others, to become emotionally close others, to take their perspective. It might involve finding a "career anchor," or a sense of identity, or it might involve developing a sense of responsibility towards the community, or a sense of what life is really about. Similarly, the sense of lineage and ancestry frequently provides people with a sense of meaning.

The life task is both broader and deeper than the "life chore." A life chore might be something like: pass an exam, buy a house, get a job, sell my car, join a club, and settle in a new town. These chores are the subassemblies that, when put together form the life task, which is an overarching direction of a life, comprised of a group of smaller, but important "chores" or sub-tasks.

The family is a system composed of individuals having disparate life tasks. These life tasks have the effect of both pulling the family together and of pulling it apart. (In more conceptual language, the impact has both centrifugal and centripetal effects.) Somehow all of this, if the family is to remain reasonably functional, has to be coordinated.

As an example, we might imagine a family that is comprised as follows:

Father, 45 years old—life task— helping the next generation to grow

Mother, 33 years old—life task—finding a solid career anchor.

Son, 15 years old—life task—finding a meaningful interpersonal identity.

Daughter, 5 years old—life task—mastering symbol systems and social interaction through play.

Grandmother, 74 years old—life task—maintaining a sense of integrity and meaning in the face of illness and death.

A moment's reflection on this family will lead us to realize that at times they might not always "get along," while at others they may "get along very well" as they pursue their life tasks. When the father helps the children to grow he may feel very satisfied, just as they feel that their life tasks are being furthered. (Of course people rarely think, "Great, my life tasks are being furthered!" but the argument here is that at some level, unconsciously, precisely this realization does take place, with encouraging results, in most cases). On the other hand, for example, the son, in finding his personal identity, will probably feel that he has to slough off the identity offered to him by his parents as not being truly his. This can lead to experiences of conflict and frustration. We have just started to examine the many tensions and harmonies that might arise from this group of five individuals trying to realize their life tasks together.

The life task framework is a useful template for analyzing the dynamics of family life. Thus, an entire chapter will be spent on this perspective.

Activity 13:
Think of a family. List the members of the family and their corresponding life tasks. Identify two "harmonies" (that is, ways in which the life tasks help people interact with one another) and two tensions that arise from these disparate life tasks. Finally, write a sentence or two about how these tensions are resolved in this family.

Members and their life tasks:

Harmonies:
1.

2.

Tensions:
1.

2.

How the family copes with these tensions.

Now let us move on to the last of the eight domains of social systems. We have examined: fantasies, phantasies, feelings, boundaries, authority, roles and tasks. Last, but not least are the rules that the family (or any social system) adopts to govern these domains.

Rules—All systems have rules that govern their operation. Much like a soccer game, the system is defined by its rules and the relationship the individuals have to the rules of the system. If there are no rules, then there is no game, the system and the meaning that was derived from the game or system also collapses. Our sense of meaning is tied to rules and our observance (or non-observance) of them.

Rules interact with all of the other components we have dealt with so far. Rules govern roles. Rules are issued with varying degrees of authority. Rules set boundaries around systems and behavior. Rules govern what feelings are permissible in a social system or what tasks the family should concern itself with. Rules bind with every component of family life and define its nature. They are the keystone to the family arch, guiding its forces so as to delimit its form.

Rules not only have domains, that is, areas of concern, (such as those we have just outlined), they also have other qualities. By taking note of these we can gain many useful insights into family functioning. First, rules can be more *explicit* or more *implicit*. Some rules are "out there" in the open, public and clearly stated. For example "All people under eighteen must be home by 10:00 p.m. on school-nights" is explicit, public and clear. "Do not use that tone of voice with me!" is explicit, but perhaps less clear in that the "tone of voice" is sometimes hard to define, you just know it when you hear it. Other rules are implicit, and mysterious, for example, a family could have a rule like, "Do not talk about Daddy's older brother." They could observe this rule without ever knowing how or why or by whom it was set. They might not even know, until it was pointed out to them, that they indeed had this rule. These types of rules are extremely tricky in families because they often have a powerful effect on functioning and at the same time are difficult to discuss. Thus the *discussability* of a rule emerges as another important dimension of rules in family systems (in fact in all social systems).

If a rule is discussable then it is more open to change. Families and social systems, if they are to survive, will probably need to change in order to adapt to an ever-changing external and internal environment. Thus, rendering rules discussable, in theory, at least, renders the system more open to change, makes it more open and more able to meet its primary tasks in an changing world. This principle of discussability runs into several barriers, however. One is that rendering a rule discussable will often be experienced as a reduction in the authority or power of the rule maker. Often the rule-maker or makers will resist discussing a rule in order to maintain the status quo and the power they have. Another is that rules are frequently held to be undiscussable so that the anxieties the undicussability conceals remain under wraps. For example, someone in the family above might say, "Why don't we ever talk about Uncle Bob, Daddy's older brother?" The anxiety level goes up in the family and unless the questioner is very persistent, naïve or a professional family therapist, the issue will probably be dropped. Implicit rules often act like rituals in societies. They are there to bind and conceal anxiety, but the fact that that is their function has long since been forgotten.

Activity 14:
Think of a family you know. Write down a) three explicit rules it seems to operate on, b) three implicit rules it seems to have, and c) comment on the level of discussability of the rules in this family.

A)   Three explicit rules:
1.

2.

3.

B)   Three implicit rules:
1.

2.

3.

C. Discussability of rules in this family:

As a way of tying all this complexity together and getting a feeling for how this might apply to a family, this activity should serve as a good "culminating event" for this chapter.

Activity 15:
Think of a family (perhaps yours). In each of the sections below write a sentence or two describing how your family is operating in each of the task domains. Next write what changes might be beneficial for this family.

1.   **Economic security**
   a.   *How this family operates.*

   b.   *How it might change.*

2.   **Socialization**
   a.   *How this family operates.*

   b.   *How it might change.*

3.   **Sexuality**
   a.   *How this family operates.*

   b.   *How it might change.*

4.   **Reality Testing**
   a.   *How this family operates.*

   b.   *How it might change.*

5. **Attachment**
   a. **How this family operates.**

   b. **How it might change.**

6. **Emotional Support**
   a. **How this family operates.**

   b. **How this family might change.**

   7. **Stability**
   a. **How this family operates.**

   b. **How this family might change.**

8. **Meaning-Purpose**
   a. **How this family operates.**

   b. **How it might change.**

9. **Psychosocial-Emotional Development**
   a. **How this family operates.**

   b. **How this family might change.**

10. Concluding remarks
As I look over my observations here, I come up with following ideas....

      a.

      b.

      c.

This chapter has dealt with families as social systems. Throughout, we have started off with the abstract properties of systems language and attempted to link this with the everyday practicalities of family life. The systems viewpoint provides us with a mind-set that helps reveal dynamics in families that might ordinarily escape our notice. In the next chapter we pick up on and amplify a theme that was touched on in Chapter One, namely the family as a cauldron of human development. It was stated that the family is where we do most of our growth, development and repair. If this assertion is reasonably true, we will need some templates of human growth and development if we are to understand more fully the internal dynamics of families. After an examination of a case example, that is where we will be going next.

Case Study 1
"Ordinary People"

The movie, "Ordinary People" beautifully depicts many of the concepts covered so far. It also demonstrates many of the ideas to be covered in upcoming sections. Let us walk through the movie and show how the eight aspects of social systems connect with it.

The film concerns an upper middle class family that lives in a north shore suburb of Chicago. A son, Buck, has recently died in a boating accident. The younger son, Conrad, when we join the movie, has recently gotten out of hospital after a suicide attempt. The movie follows the family over a period of months as it attempts to deal with the aftermath of these shocks.

In no way can the following application of concepts be exhaustive. It is intended only to provide an example of how some of the concepts covered so far might apply to a family.

Activity 16:
Watch the film "Ordinary People." Answer the questions below.

1. *Draw a diagram of this family as a system.*

   What does this image reveal?

2. *What is the recent stressful event for this family?*

3. *How are individuals in the family dealing with this?*

   Who seems to be carrying most of the "symptoms"?

4. *Is this an open family system? What leads you to this conclusion?*

5. *How does the culture of this family's (upper-middle class, "Anglo Saxon") community affect it?*

6. *What is the role of the therapist?*

7. *What are the roles each family member plays?*

8. *What seems to bring on changes at the end of the narrative?*

9. *What non-verbal communication and body language do you see?*

Fantasies

The family is full of fantasies, both conscious and unconscious. Beth the, mother, spends time in Buck's old room in a twilight state, observing all of his trophies and wall hangings. It seems that she has not fully accepted his death, that she imagines he is still alive.

When the parents are asked how Conrad, their distressed son is doing, they reply that he is just great, as if their wish that he be well supersedes the reality if his obvious disturbance.

Conrad has the focal fantasy that he in some way was responsible for his brother's death. This fantasy interferes with his mourning. Calvin, the father, states that when Beth buried Buck, her favorite son, it was as if part of her died with him, touching on the fantasy of a physical unity between the mother and her first born son.

This is a small sampling of the fantasies we find operating in a very potent fashion, often in the underworld of this family.

Affect/Feeling

The emotional life of this family is very telling. First, we can see that there is a restriction on the intensity of emotions that are expressed. In addition there seems to be a prohibition with regard to the expression of anger. In an early scene, we can see that Beth is clearly angered by Conrad's refusal to eat breakfast. She says nothing, but forcefully pushes the French toast down the garbage disposal, shakes off the feelings and moves on. Conrad believes his mother hates him for some imagined complicity in the death of Buck, but this emotion, when it is finally brought out into the open, is vigorously denied.

A turning point occurs in the life of the family when Conrad has an angry outburst, yelling, "Give her the goddamn camera!" Disruptive as this expression of rage is, it seems to give the family some room to breathe.

Similar difficulties seem to exist in the expression of tender emotions. Late in the movie, Conrad hugs and kisses his mother. She responds stiffly, mannequin-like.

Boundaries

This family is perhaps over bound, meaning that its functionality is compromised by the boundaries between its subsystems and its environment being too impermeable. On the positive side this shows up as the father respectfully knocking on Conrad's door. On the other hand, Conrad states that he missed having his father "haul his ass," and take him to task— perhaps keeping too much distance between them.

We also see that the parents, Beth and Calvin, have different notions regarding the permeability of the external family boundary. Calvin quite blithely shares with a woman at a party that their son is seeing a psychiatrist.

On the way home, Beth is very angered at this display of "dirty laundry," concerned about what others might think.

Authority

We see that Beth and Calvin have different notions regarding parental authority. After a blow-up with his mother, Conrad storms upstairs. Calvin goes to follow and Beth feels betrayed, thinking that this means Calvin is giving in to Conrad. Calvin says that he is not giving in, he simply wants to understand. Calvin's position seems to be that authority can be maintained along with emotional contact, while Beth seems to believe that authority relies on emotional distance. This is in turn connected to other differences that emerge between them.

Roles

Calvin, the father, plays the informal role of "peacemaker" or "placator." He wants to avoid conflict and have everyone get along. This seems to conflict at times with other paternal functions of discipline, although we do see him at time taking up the role of concerned advisor, coach and persuader.

Beth, the mother, plays the role of "traffic cop." She directs the flow of conversation, changing the subject subtly or not so subtly when it displeases her.

Conrad plays the role of "patient." He carries and contains most of the distress in the family. In this way, he also plays the role of "whipping boy" ,"scapegoat" or "sin eater."

As the movie develops we see a changing of roles. This is especially true of Conrad as, with the help of a therapist, he gets more in touch with his repressed feelings, processes his trauma and engages in the "working through" of his mourning his brother. As the roles shift, so a crisis emerges in the family. The balance or equilibrium is upset. Participants are called upon to shift roles. At the end of the movie, we are left with the question, "How much will these ordinary people be able to change?"

Task

On the surface this family is achieving its tasks. Certainly they are materially very comfortable. They have wealth, a comfortable house, a nice school, nice clothes, enough food and seem well accepted in the community. However, the task they face of mourning the loss of their son is not proceeding very well at all. This is a case of complicated mourning at the level of the family. All the components discussed thus far conspire to make the accomplishment of this task very difficult. It is hard to mourn in an environment where feelings are not to be expressed, or fantasies explored. Thus this task, the difficult and painful task of working through the sudden violent loss (and sudden violent losses are more difficult to mourn) of a son is at a standstill.

Paradoxically, people will sometimes respond to a loss such as this with a spurt of emotional growth. While the loss is initially devastating, people can, after a while, emerge from the loss changed, deeper and more complex, with a vastly enriched being. This seems to be happening in the family, where Calvin and Conrad, at the end seem to be embarked on a new life. For Beth, we are less sure as to whether she will grow or stagnate in a tragically empty and split-off way.

With regard to the life developmental tasks—the topic we take up in the next chapter, we can see that Conrad's adolescent tasks of finding an identity and young adult tasks of achieving an intimate relationship (tasks ascribed to these eras by Erik Erikson—see next chapter) come to a grinding halt as he deals with the PTSD (Post Traumatic Stress Disorder) and complicated mourning engendered by his brother's death. As he resolves these issues, we see him make and break some commitments, in an effort to find himself, and we see his relationship to "Pratt," his girlfriend, develop and deepen.

The same disruption of life task development can be seen in the parents, who seem awash in stagnation, to use Erikson's chilling but felicitous term. Again, as the family begins to resolve the issues of loss we see Calvin come alive around his generative contact with his son. Beth, however, is more of a question mark. Will she remain hidden behind her bourgeois mask, or will she develop the capacity for more authentic generative living? It seems like a long and difficult path lies before her.

Rules

"Rules"; the concept threads through the previous paragraphs. This family is redolent with rules—rules regarding the display of feelings, the making of messes, the communication of information, who is to touch whom, what tone of voice to use, what topics are permissible for conversation. The list goes on. We see how when one of these rules is challenged or changed, the entire system is altered. When Conrad breaks a rule regarding expression of anger, a crisis is created. When Calvin breaks an unwritten rule and asks Beth why she was so concerned about the appropriateness of his attire on the day of Buck's funeral, another crisis is engendered and the system alters.

The therapist, to some extent, in this movie, plays the role of "instigator" insofar as he challenges Conrad to alter his rules of operation, and this enters the family, causing it to change.

Conclusion

The movie "Ordinary People" concerns an imaginary family, and yet, like all good art, it springs to life and engages us as if it was "real." In many ways all families are imaginary insofar as they involve fantasies, both conscious and unconscious. Thus exploring even imaginary families can be extremely useful in our studies. Furthermore, imaginary families, when they embody the systems concepts we have examined so far, do spring into life, as if they are real. This liveliness, although, it does not "prove" the truthfulness of the systems approach, does lend it a good deal of warranted assertibility (to use John Dewey's useful term).

CHAPTER 2
The Family as a Crucible of Growth

This chapter continues with one of the assertions in the previous chapter, that the family serves as the place where people accomplish their life-task developmental goals. It is the family that supports us and challenges us and provides the means whereby we may grow emotionally and psycho-socially. This chapter provides a template for understanding this assertion and charting the course of human development as it takes place in the supportive matrix of the family.

It was asserted in Chapter One that humans and human systems are pre-programmed, "hard wired" to grow—to increase in complexity. In this chapter we explore the sequences in which this growth might occur. There are a plethora of theories regarding human growth and development. For the purposes of this text, we will simply select elements of a few that, together, provide a useful "roadmap" of development across the life course. The first of these theories is that of Erik Erikson—his "epigenetic life cycle."

Erikson's Eight Stages of Life

Erik Erikson provides us with a theory that is at one sweep complex, yet easy to understand, simple, yet based on multicultural observations and anthropological research. It is a time-honored theory, and yet it is remarkably durable. This presentation of his theory will in no way do justice to the breadth and depth of Erikson's usually underestimated theory. It will only relate the essentials of his ideas so that we may bring together a scheme of development and family systems—in itself a complex task.

The table below outlines the eight stages, the approximate ages in which these concerns are priorities, the virtues, or psychosocial strengths that emerge from the successful completion of each stage, the ritualization or activities that promote development in each given stage and the distortion that arises when the life task is not successfully mastered.

Erikson's Eight Life Stages

Stage	Age	Virtue	Ritualization	Distortion
TRUST-MISTRUST	1ST Yr	HOPE	RECOGNITION	IDOLISM
AUTONOMY-SHAME, DOUBT	2ND Yr	WILL	JUDGMENTS	PREJUDICE
INITIATIVE-GUILT	3-5 Yrs	PURPOSE	DRAMA-PLAY	IMPERSONATION
INDUSTRY-INFERIORITY RITUAL	5-12Yrs	COMPETENCE	FORMAL	EMPTY RITUAL
IDENTITY-ROLE CONFUSION	12-25Yrs	FIDELITY	IDEOLOGY	TOTALISM
INTIMACY-ISOLATION	20-40Yrs	MUTUALITY	AFFILIATION	ELITISM
GENERATIVITY-STAGNATION	40-Old Age	CARE	GENERATIONAL	AUTHORITISM
EGO INTEGRITY-DESPAIR	Old Age	WISDOM	ETERNAL TRUTHS	SAPIENTISM

Each stage of Erikson's theory involves a dialectic, a creative tension between two opposites. The developmental task involves creatively integrating these opposite poles of experience in such a way that one develops enough of the "virtue" or psychological strength to enable the tackling of the next stage. One is challenged, in each stage to achieve a balance between the two poles that are at the forefront for that era of life. The balance that is required by society will vary depending on the society one is living in. Some societies will have cultures, for example, that will emphasize a higher level of "mistrust," or another society may inculcate and "require" a higher level of, say, "guilt." The reader is referred to Erikson's works to gain further insight into these processes.

The stages are sequential and inter-related. For example, the achievement of Intimacy in stage six clearly will rest on the degree one learned to trust in the first stage. The ease with which one establishes an identity in stage five will rest in part on how much of a sense of initiative and competence was developed in stages three and four. It is a good example of an integrated system.

While the stages are sequential, one is always dealing with all the issues throughout one's entire life. Little children often have very wise insights, and similarly old people deal with issues of trust along with the many other concerns of childhood. The whole table is alive in us all the time. What Erikson is positing is that certain issues or dilemmas move into the foreground during certain periods of life, giving it a developmental stamp. Indeed if this were not the case there would be little chance for us to rework old issues or to understand one another across generations.

This is not a lock step pre-programmed package. That would mean life was very boring and predictable. The framework is perhaps best viewed as a creative plaything, which can, if used flexibly, help us chart meaningful pathways through the labyrinth of life. Furthermore, I shall, in the following account, integrate several ideas from attachment theory and recent infant research.

The columns on the chart refer, of course to the eight stages of life—from birth to death. The ages on the second column are approximate. They may stretch or compress, depending on the culture we are operating in. They are especially flexible in adulthood, where issues like life expectancy and physical health can intervene and expand one's middle age or, unexpectedly bring on old age and death quite early.

The column "Virtues" refers to the psycho-social strength that develops as a result of successfully mastering the conflict inherent in each stage. This virtue or strength enables one to move on to the next life task and forms an integral part of the developing personality. Different cultures will place different values on the virtues depending on the adaptations the culture has to make to its environment.

The column "Ritualization" refers to the developmental activities that the individual must participate in if they are to master the stage successfully, if they are to integrate the opposite poles of the stage and if they are to develop the virtue of the stage. It is tantamount to the "work" the individual must do if they are to accomplish the life task. This concept will become clearer as we progress through the stages, and as I provide examples.

The column "Distortion" refers to the warping of the personality that will occur if the individual is prevented in some way from adequately accomplishing the developmental task of that stage—if they are unable to integrate, to balance, to "make sense of" the dilemma that stage confronts them with.

It is an interesting theory, despite valid feminist critiques (Gilligan 1982). According to Erikson, we always have some work to do. In this he is close to his theoretical forebear, Freud, who claimed that life was all about love and work and believed that the human being was riven with conflicts. Erikson takes Freud's theory and places it in a social milieu and thus transforms

Freud's *psychosexual* theory into a *psychosocial* theory. Let us walk through the stages of this theory, remembering that all of this development occurs in, and is promulgated and supported by, the *family*.

Trust and Mistrust

During the first year of life the baby (soon to be a toddler) is in a state of extreme dependence on others. Will they come when he needs them? Will they respond to his needs for food, warmth, nurturance and social contact? Will the caretakers understand when he is too cold, or tired, or over-stimulated; when she is bored or irritated by clothing; when she is having trouble swallowing or has pains? Anyone who has been around a baby for an hour or so knows that they are in frequent need of attention and understanding of this sort. The question the baby has is, "Can these caretakers be trusted to show up on time and will they get it right? Will they understand me, minister to my needs and make me feel o.k. again?" Recall that the baby does not have speech yet and is in a state of absolute dependence. Failures in the caretaking system arguably confront the baby with a fear of dying and with deep dreads that cannot be communicated in words. The types of trust we are discussing here are very basic in that they deal with survival, going on being. Some "failures" are inevitable. Adults are not omniscient. Sometimes they cannot get to the baby quickly enough. Sometimes they cannot take the pain away. If these failures are not too severe, then the infant's sense of basic trust, their sense that others (and by extension, they themselves) are trustworthy is left reasonably intact. If not, a deep sense of mistrust is formed at the very foundation of the personality, making the mastery of later stages more difficult. Very important in the acquisition of this sense of basic trust is a **secure attachment** wherein the infant develops a sense of security from a warm, sensitive and empathic relationship with one or several caretakers.

The upshot of this basic trust is the psychological strength (or "virtue," as Erikson calls it) of *hope*. The fact that the caretakers have "come through" in a reasonably tolerable way has laid down a belief that has become generalized, that even when things get bad, they will soon, or eventually, get better.

Recall that the ritualization for this stage is "recognition." The ritualization is an activity that the individual needs to repeat over and over again in order to gain mastery of the tasks of that stage. "Recognition" here means that the baby comes to recognize many patterns and repeated stimuli in its world. It recognizes its caretakers, perhaps at first by their smell, later on by recognizing their faces. Babies will recognize sequences of events around daily occurrences—feeding sequences, bathing, going to sleep, leaving the house, nursing and so on. Caretakers who remain stable and familiar, or who pace themselves in the way they present themselves so the baby can recognize them, or who speak in tones that help babies recognize meaning and connections between tones, sounds and other events aid babies in the task of recognition. Repetitive games also help recognition—games like "peek-a-boo" play on the emerging capacity of the baby to recognize faces and voices. Mothers and other caretakers who, in their "conversations" with babies manifest recognition, an understanding of their feeling states and physical conditions, help babies recognize their own feelings and sensations, make sense of them and develop a sense of self-trust that is based on self understanding.

Finally, if the baby has the great misfortune of not having caretakers whom they can trust or importantly if they had other experiences that disrupted their sense of their own and the world's basic trustworthiness, for example through having had a painful illness, or a surgical procedure, or a separation from loved ones, then a *distortion* in the foundation of the personality might occur. Sometimes this distortion might result from something happening in the life or the mind of the parents that, as it were, comes through and affects the baby. The mother might be suffering from a deep depression such that, try as she might, she cannot make herself as emotionally available to her baby as she would like. Perhaps the father suffers a career setback, or a grandmother, who was acting as an important emotional backup for the parents suddenly dies. These factors, distant and unrelated though they might seem at first blush, can have serious effects on the baby, even more so, if they are underestimated, ignored and not compensated for in some other way. These extensions of the possibilities lead us away from the pernicious trap of "blaming the mother, or father." Recall that we are taking a systemic approach here—causality is distributed—small effects in one part of the system can be amplified in other regions of the system, oftentimes with unanticipated consequences. Further, there is much research to suggest that infants are born with different temperaments (some being for example, easy to "warm up or console" and others being more difficult to soothe) and with different thresholds for pain, irritation and allergic responses. What for one baby is just a minor annoyance from which they can easily be retrieved is for another infant terrible pain from which it is hard to recover. These factors also interact with personality features of parents and can either result in strain (if parents can take things in their stride) or in a derailment, temporary or long term, of the parent-infant relationship (if, for example, the parents are prone to feeling guilty or have difficulty in coping with stress). In addition, physical differences in the infant can cause derailing of caretaker-baby relationships. For example if the baby has a palate that makes swallowing difficult, the feeding experience can result in a fear of choking, frustration and hunger.

The distortion of *idolism* can be understood as the person seeking that certain someone or something that can be trusted absolutely. This quest, which was not adequately realized in the first year of life, is then pursued during later stages, when it is much harder to realize or can get the individual into difficulty, as when, say, cult members idolize their leader. Sometimes this need can be institutionalized and organized in such a way as to take away many of the social risks, in such institutions as are developed around religious leaders. Idolism is a carry over of infantile yearning, and while everyone arguably has a "piece" of this in us (that is probably an active element in love—both requited and unrequited), too much can seriously impair the individual's chances of resolving the developmental dilemmas of later stages.

Activity 17:
Observe an infant (under the age of 12 months) for at least 20 minutes. Take notes. Review the notes. Do you see elements of Erikson's ideas? Write down which ones and how they showed in your observations.

What else did you observe? What did you learn? What questions are you left with?

Autonomy and Shame, Self-Doubt

As the child moves into the second year of life, he or she becomes more independent. They have more of "a mind of their own." One can observe this in simple everyday events. When we try to put clothes on a six-month old, the baby is usually compliant, bending to the will of the adult—they certainly do not argue about color or style. By the time eighteen months rolls around, putting on clothes is different. It can become a battle of wills. Perhaps the toddler isn't ready to get dressed right now, or she doesn't want to wear a party dress or the down coat. Perhaps there is even a tantrum because a certain material is too scratchy or a dress is "ugly." Feeding will have changed too. The child will probably have "tastes" and preferences and will refuse to eat certain things or to use certain utensils. The child, by the end of the second year, has learned how to use the word "NO!"

In all of this the child is expressing their emerging autonomy, their capacity for self-direction. Of course, parents usually want their children to be self-directed. Although this wish will vary from individual to individual, family to family and culture to culture, the pathway to self-direction is not always convenient. Conflicts of will are bound to arise. Parents are likely to induce shame and self-doubt in the child as a means of gaining the upper hand. They may say things like, "Don't use that tone with *me!*" or "Shame on you!" or, "Bad boy! Nasty!" or "If you do that one more time..."

These bring on a sense of shame or self-doubt in the child. In each family, a balance will be struck. In some cases, the emphasis may be on the shame end of the spectrum—perhaps so much so that the child develops a paralysis of their will or gives up all shame completely and becomes "shameless" in the way they impose their will on others. This latter can be often seen in children who are abused and grow up to be tyrants or bigots. In other families the resolution might be at the autonomy end of the spectrum, and the child is encouraged to "do their own thing" untrammeled by feelings of shame or self-doubt. Oftentimes this occurs when the parents feel uncertain of their authority or guilty about setting limits. These children may develop anxiety around the limitations of their will, they may feel unprotected in such an unbounded environment and, deep down, they may have an awareness that somehow they are not learning about social limits and how to "fit in," how to "go along with the program" even when it involves bending one's own will to the will of others.

This clearly can be a tricky phase of development. A lot is at stake. Parents usually want their children to be autonomous and to have a strong will, but they also do not want their children to run roughshod over others. How to balance this? Our willpower can take us lots of places; it can help us do amazing things, but it can also harm others. Deep questions indeed!

The ritualization of this stage is *judgment.* In this, Erikson is arguing that the way the child learns to integrate the opposite poles of autonomy and shame is by making decisions, by working through, in a toddler fashion, dilemmas and judgmental processes. This again can be seen in the everyday events in the family—the toddler is asked to choose what he would like to eat, to select a shirt to wear, to contribute to the decisions about what colors to use. This process is also tied up with the development of language that is proceeding apace during this epoch. Things are put in categories. "Dog," says the child. "No, Shetland pony," says the adult. Judgment is also seen in the toddler's interest in sorting things.

When the child is not afforded the opportunity to participate in decisions, then the process of judgment-making is short-circuited, and becomes very primitive. It becomes prejudice, where decisions are made, typically about things that are good and bad, but in a very simplistic and closed fashion. The process whereby the toddler is excluded from decision making (or is overwhelmed by having to make "decisions" that are way in advance of their capacities is usually saturated with the experience of shame. This shame is then defensively projected into a "bad other" (thing or person) about which one maintains prejudicial negative attitudes.

One can see here, at the outset, how, if a child enters the second phase with a mistrustful attitude (stemming from experiences in the first year) and this combines with the distortion of prejudice, resulting from overwhelming experiences of shame and self-doubt in the second phase, we can have a personality that is already, at age two, primed for paranoid prejudice. A cursory look at the newspapers or the history books can demonstrate how costly this combination can be.

Finally, a paradoxical note. Imagine a child who is extremely fortunate in its first year and develops a very trusting attitude. This child, upon reaching the second year of life, may feel so secure that they really push the boundaries and are quite the risk-taker in exerting their will, not as fearful as another child who is not so secure. This reminds me of the saying by D.W. Winnicott, (a well-known pediatrician and psychoanalyst) to the effect that health in a child is more difficult to deal with than illness. When a child is anxious, insecure and depressed, they are more easily oppressed and frightened into compliance. When they are none of these, they are more liable to be spontaneous and take the parental world by surprise.

68

Activity 17:
Observe a toddler between 1 and 2 years old for about half an hour. Take notes. Are there at least two correspondences between what Erikson posits and what you observe?

A.

B.

What else do you observe? What are its potential impacts on the family?

Initiative and Guilt

By the time the child reaches the age of three, much psychological and physical growth has occurred. One key development is in the domain of memory. Children, by the time they are three or four have developed a memory bank of experiences that they can, as it were, "pull up" into their conscious minds. They can then use these memories to fashion action plans that extend for some time into the future. At first these action plans may be quite short and simple, like, "Let us go to the park and buy an ice cream!" but they soon enough will become extended and complex, like, "Let us take the tea tray out of the cupboard and use it as a sled to slide down the stairs." They become able to chain together action sequences together in ways that are new and creative. Of course much of the time this will be charming and wonderfully expansive, but at others it will involve risk, danger to self or others or damage to property. The family, along with the individual, faces a dilemma—a dilemma with far reaching social consequences—a dilemma that stays with us all of our lives, but which is particularly prominent during the years of three to five. This dilemma involves balancing one's initiative—one's "get up and go!" with the potential harm one can do by simply doing one's own thing. This may sound similar to the previous stage, and in some ways it is. The key difference has to do with the time sense and the complexity of the plans. This can be seen when we look at the different types of arguments that go on between two year olds and adults and four year olds and adults. With the two year old, it is a "timeless" battle of wills—"Yes!" versus "No!" With a four year old, it is possible to negotiate, to make plans like, "Okay, we will go to the park, but first we clean your room and I have to run some errands." It is also possible to point out to the child simple consequences of their actions. The "will" of the previous stage has elaborated into a sense of purpose. Purposes can be very good things. John Dewey, the pragmatist philosopher holds that, "freedom is the capacity to frame one's purposes and carry them into effect." To the extent that Dewey and Erikson are correct, this period of life is crucial in the individual's sense of freedom. On the other hand, when we exercise our freedom we can hurt others. When we become aware of this we feel guilt. Too much guilt and we lose our initiative; too little and we run roughshod over others. How to balance this? This is the dilemma the individual and the family face during this epoch. And these are high stakes indeed—initiative, purpose, guilt, social responsibility, ambition—lives are made and broken on such reefs.

The distortion that can result from an imbalance in this era is that of *impersonation.* If the child experiences too high a "dosage" of guilt, there is the risk that he or she might become very compliant, and, instead of acting upon their own purposes, they act upon their idea of what the parents' purposes are. They might become a "little adult" and, in a disquietingly precocious manner mimic what they think the adults want to see. Perhaps all of us do this to some extent, put up a mask to please and placate the adults. To do it too much, however causes the individual to lose touch with what they really want to do. I have sometimes worked with individuals in their thirties, for example, who have quite successful careers, but feel a deep emptiness and lack of meaning. Closer inspection reveals that they chose their career, often at an early age, to placate their parents, sometimes to please them, sometimes so as not to hurt them or make them anxious. It would often take a lot of searching and psychological work for them to discover their "true self" and what purposes were truly their own.

Sometimes the distortion of impersonation may show up in a child who is a bit too "good." This child may never make a mess or say a mean word or lose control of their impulses, and is thus taken to be a model child by many adults, but underneath, the true self is being sacrificed. Alice Miller, in her book, "The Drama of the Gifted Child" gives a fine documentation of how the gifted or sensitive child can all too easily fall into this trap.

The *ritualization* of this stage is that of drama, or play. The children find out about themselves and realize their purposes through play. This is easy to see in children of this age. Their desire to play seems inexhaustible. They will play until they drop and fall asleep, literally, in their tracks. Then wake up and play some more. The topic of play is an especially important and complex one, especially for children. The focus here is on the way in which children's play can help them learn how to frame purposes and carry them into effect, to learn about reality, to co-operate with others and to learn about their limitations. Play also offers an opportunity to "think aloud," to talk oneself through action sequences. Play thus also offers terrific opportunities for self-discovery, discovery of others, and the elaboration of meaning-systems. The prescription for this period seems to be "Play, and plenty of it."

On the other hand a child who does not encounter the experience of guilt in response to some of their projects might find themselves in the unsettling position of not being able to shape their sense of purpose towards socially useful ends, or they may be beset by anxiety-producing fantasies of the results of their actions. It might be that they do not have the experience of, "There, that wasn't so bad, was it?" which can be relaxing and comforting, especially since such realizations can tame omnipotent fantasies that can engender much excitement, but more anxiety. Such children may become "paralyzed" or beset with their own primitive phantasies of guilt and retribution that have not been supplanted by well-modulated realistic experiences of guilt and the consequences of behavior.

Activity 19:
Observe a 3-6 year old child for at least 40 minutes; do you see behavior that corresponds to Erikson's theory? Yes or No?

Write an example of a typical behavior that you observed below,

What effects did the child's behavior seem to have on the family?

What effects did the family seem to have on the behavior of the child?

What questions arose from this observation?

Industry and Inferiority

The age of five or six marks a momentous shift in the lives of most children, no matter where they are. Around this age, it is as if the child is ready to be introduced to the community, to begin to learn the skills that are important in that society, to participate in the processes of production, either in reality or in a modeled way. It is as if the community picks up on this readiness in the child and starts to transmit to the child, through institutions like schools or apprenticeships, or informally, as the child follows the adult through their daily activities, the skills that are important in the culture. This may involve things like the manipulation of symbols or materials, or interaction with others. It may involve encounters with the religious systems in the culture, the artistic modalities that are used and the historical narratives common to that culture. For better or worse, the child also encounters elements in the culture that have to do with class and caste, with social groupings, cliques and prejudice. To a greater or lesser extent the task of socialization is handed over by the family to others. These others might be professionals, such as teachers, artisans or a religious leader, or they may be informal others who train or impart their knowledge. The child, for their part, leaves the drama of the family, to a greater or lesser extent, and starts living their life outside of the family, in the classroom, on the streets, in the playground, on the village green or in the fields. On the other hand, the family relinquishes, to some extent, "ownership" of the child, much as the mother has had to relinquish ownership of the child's body over the first three years or so of its life.

Learning and the gaining of competencies are of prime importance during this era. On the one hand, when we feel things are going swimmingly, and we are succeeding in gaining the skills we are faced with, be it reading, writing or arithmetic, we feel suffused with the sense of *industry*, and a concomitant feeling of *competence*—a feeling of confidence, a "can do" feeling. On the other hand when the child feels overwhelmed and unable to complete the task, there is the sense of inferiority and a vulnerable shrinking feeling of inadequacy. This is a deep feeling, one that almost anyone seems able to recall from his or her own childhood. It is deep because so much hinges on the human being's capacity to work in a group and make a valued contribution. Human beings are group animals, able only to survive in a meaningful way if they function in a group.

If the child does not achieve a sense of competence, then they are likely to "fake it" as if they know what they are up to. Erikson calls this *empty ritual*— a sort of going through the motions, to give the appearance of competence where there is little or none.

On the other hand the child might not be able to use the experience of inferiority productively, for many times a sense that one has a lot to learn can be very functional. It can help one pay attention to those who are more competent in a given field and helps preserve curiosity, ideals and ambition.

The successful integration of these two poles results in a sense of competence balanced by a readiness to learn.

Let us pause a moment and list the "virtues" that we hope we have developed by about age eleven. It is an impressive list: hope, will, purpose and competence. They will stand the soon-to-be-adolescent (and adult) in good stead in the challenges that are to come.

Activity 20:
Recall an experience from your life that had to do with;

A. Industry

B. Inferiority

How did these experiences feel? What effect did they have on you?

What changes occur in the family as the child enters the stage of industry and inferiority? For example, how do roles, feelings, fantasies and rules shift in the family system?

Identity and Identity Confusion

As we enter the stage of adolescence, we hope that a robust sense of competence has developed. Based on this confidence, we see the individual ask that vital human question, "Who am I?" In a relatively simple society, this question might be answered fairly quickly, for there might only be a relatively small array of roles that one can take up in adult life. In massive, complex, postindustrial societies, that are undergoing rapid change, the number of roles available can be enormous (especially if one comes from a privileged class) and the roles themselves are in a continuous stage of rapid flux.

At times, an adolescent may seem to settle on something as an existential anchor—perhaps a professional choice or a religious belief and they experience a sense of *identity,* of knowing who they are and where they belong. Often, however this sense of self-certainty dissolves and the uncertainty and questioning returns, along with a sense of *identity confusion,* the uncomfortable feeling of being uncertain as to who one is or where one belongs, how one might fit in with the larger world. It is a challenging period indeed—a period of finding out about the world, what possibilities it holds and of finding out about oneself, about what things are of value, of what is interesting, what makes life worthwhile. Frequently this will involve a challenge to those who define the adult world—middle-aged people. These challenges often involve *ideology*—a questioning of beliefs, values and attitudes. "Why do things have to be this way?" "Why is this wrong?" "How come you have so much power?" "How do you know what is right?" These questions and many others help an adolescent (or anyone, for that matter) find out about the world and themselves. They may be inconvenient, but they are functional for development. They are the *ritualization* for this era.

At times, it seems as though adolescents need to "take a break" from the rigors of all this effort and just float aimlessly for a while, as if they have become becalmed—not doing anything of note. These "doldrums" might be functional too, in that they can provide what Erikson called a *moratorium* –a "time out" that can be helpful in coming to terms with oneself and the roles life has to offer. Perhaps it clears a space for a lifelong organizing passion to emerge. Sometimes this moratorium can extend for a year or so, often involving travel or study. During a moratorium, adolescents "abstain" from making any serious lasting commitment—a commitment that would tie them down or "define" them for too long.

Clearly sometimes this moratorium can extend for some people into their adulthood and this can present difficulties later on. For it is commitments that bring adolescence to end—commitments to others, to a religion, to a career, to oneself, to one's family, community, to a political creed, to a set of ideals—these organize and solidify identity—they give a feeling of being someone with a set of attributes or qualities.

It can happen, under unfortunate circumstances, and for a dizzying array of reasons, that individuals make commitments very quickly, early in adolescence so as to preclude the anxiety and uncertainty of identity confusion. They may "marry early," either a person or a career or a set of beliefs, and hold on to this marriage for dear life in order to gain a sense of personal solidity. This is called *identity foreclosure*. In my experience, it is not uncommon for the person to have to deal with unresolved issues of identity at a later point in their life, perhaps at the "age thirty transition," often during the "midlife crisis" (some time between 35 and 45 years old).

On the other hand, some adolescents have extreme difficulty in finding any lasting identity, even the prosthetic one offered in the form of identity foreclosure. These individuals suffer from *identity diffusion*—which is an extreme form of identity confusion, where the individual lacks a focus to their personality, and is deeply confused, even as to their gender identity.

These two extremes of difficulty in achieving a secure sense of identity demonstrate a need the adolescent has—a need for an environment that is free enough for experimentation with different roles, but safe enough so as not to cost too dearly when experiments fail or when mistakes are made. Identity is being formed here—an identity that may endure for a lifetime. Unfortunate incidents regarding labeling of the individual can result in "negative identity." It seems that people need an identity so badly, that they will opt for a negative one rather than have none at all. Thus if an experience provides for a readily available negative identity, the individual is liable to "glom on" to it with particular adhesiveness during this stage. For example, if an adolescent is labeled as a "delinquent" or a "patient," these identities may prove very difficult indeed to outgrow.

The period of early adolescence is also a period when a "normative regression" occurs. This means that, as part of the ordinary part of growing up, during adolescence many of the unresolved issues of childhood will resurface. It seems that this is potentiated by the powerful reorganization of the personality that is brought on by puberty. Thus we will often see, especially in early adolescence, periods of babyish behavior, scatological humor, tantrums and "silliness," as long repressed childhood complexes emerge into the edges of awareness. These are usually temporary and should present no serious problem, if, on the whole, the young person is moving ahead in their projects. Sometimes, however, these repressed memories are of such a powerful and painful nature that they can, as it were, suck the individual under and they become very confused. At this point it is crucial that support be provided to help in working these returning issues through. Early adolescence is one of life's several "second chances." If we are lucky, we can get a chance for a fresh start. Too frequently the support is not available for the individual to make good use of these "second chances."

Most individuals, we hope, are able to secure a relatively secure sense of identity, (and it is often relative, for many of the commitments that bring adolescence to an end are provisional commitments: often the individual knows that they will not hold them for their whole life, they will do for the "time being"). However, for those who cannot do this they may turn to the *distortion* of this era *totalism*, and give their identity over to someone or something that provides them with an identity. They may join a "cult-like organization," often with a charismatic leader. The organization will often have a dependency culture or a "fight-flight," paranoid culture and these serve to shore up the individuals' crumbling sense of who they are. Perhaps it is also buttressed by the use of code language, uniforms and a strict hierarchy, along with a sense of us against them—all this giving a sense of boundaries that the individual is unable to provide for themselves. Many "street gangs" seem to serve this function.

These paragraphs should convey the vitality, vulnerability and importance of this stage. In many ways, it is a testing ground for the previous tasks. But perhaps the biggest test of all comes in the next stage, where the very sense of identity is placed at risk in the establishment of a deep and intimate relationship.

Much recent research on gender difference has focused on the different socialization of males and females in this culture. One of the major assertions of this research is that girls tend to find their identities *through* relationships with others, while boys tend to find their identities by *differentiating* themselves from others. These different developmental pathways lead to the stereotypical relationship tensions that we observe emerging especially in young adulthood.

Recall that much of this development is occurring in the family. Relationships shift dramatically over the course of this era. At the outset, the young adolescent is quite dependent on the parents. By the end they may have already left home and be self-supporting. This stage is also, as we shall see in upcoming sections powerfully influenced by culture and technology. Libraries have been filled on these topics. We have hardly touched the surface here, but we must move on.

Activity 21:
Recall your own adolescence. Write in a memory from your early, middle and late adolescence. If you can, compare them with several others. What patterns do you see? What were the implications for you family?

A.   **Memory from early adolescence (about 12 years old)**

B.   **Memory from middle adolescence (about 15 years old)**

C.   **Memory from late adolescence (about 20 years old)**

D.   **What patterns do I see?**

E.   **What implications does this have for the family?**

Intimacy and Isolation

As we make commitments and solidify, albeit in a provisional way, our identities, we cross a very significant boundary in the course of life. We leave our *family of origin* and move towards our *family of creation.* This transition can be very stressful. In fact, in my early research on the experience of emptiness, I found that there was a significant increase in the frequency of this often-distressing feeling during the early adult years—the early twenties. This is a truly liminal period. One is crossing a threshold, and thresholds are often vulnerable ambiguous places. The next task we face will be that of establishing an intimate relationship. For those who have reasonably well achieved the previous life tasks, this may flow reasonably smoothly. For others it may be extremely difficult and there will be prolonged painful experiences of *isolation.* If this loneliness is protracted and intractable then the individual may turn to the distortion of this era as a means of annulling the pain. They may develop an *elitist* attitude. As if to make up for the pain of loneliness and the ensuing despair, they adopt the attitude that they are better than others. Perhaps they think they have a better education, or live in a nicer apartment, wear brand-name clothes, have finer stereos, automobiles or religious beliefs—as if these will numb or compensate for what is really missing in their lives, a deep sense of closeness with another human being—a sense of closeness that recapitulates some of the closeness of early infancy and provides a bonding strong enough to establish the core of a future family. Often, the elitist attitude will hold the individual for a decade, perhaps longer. Often, it will give way as the person reaches the age thirty transition, or if not then, at midlife, revealing an underworld of sadness, emptiness and despair.

The *ritualization* of this era is *affiliation,* or in plain language, "hanging out," frequenting places where one is likely to meet that certain someone with whom one may be intimate. This procedure varies (as do all of these stages) from culture to culture. In some cultures this ritualization is done through "dating"; in others, through "courting." Some cultures have marriages that are arranged to varying degrees. Some will use chaperones, while in others; it will be less well-monitored by the elders. Even the importance of romantic love varies from culture to culture. In some, it is regarded as the sole basis for a lasting intimate relationship; in others, mutual respect and duty might be more important. We shall examine these factors later.

A moment's reflection reveals just how much of a testing ground this era can be for the individual. Try to think of establishing an intimate relationship without the previously developed psychological strengths: hope, will, purpose, competence, and identity. It will be very difficult. This, the first stage of adulthood is a severe test indeed of one's previous psychosocial accomplishments. It is my opinion that this fact contributes to such things as the significant rise in the frequency of illnesses such as schizophrenia during the early twenties. For it is not only in the realm of relationships that the person is facing monumental new life tasks, there also looms the other great challenge of young adulthood: one's career. Just as one is in a liminal state in the realm of relationships, so one is on the border with regards to career, just beginning to gain access (we hope) to the career lattice and pathways of the adult world.

It is unfortunate, in my opinion, that western culture idealizes this period of life, according it the pride of place as being the "best years of your life." For many people this is a period of great tension, stress, uncertainty and struggle. To live this out in a culture that is saturated with messages that convey that this should be a period of unalloyed joy only serves to increase psychological pain and feelings of inadequacy.

Activity 21:
Think about a person between the ages of 20 and 35. Answer the following questions:

A. **Does their main priority seem to be the establishment of an intimate relationship with one other person?**

B. **Does the fact that they are male or female seem to have an effect on how they achieve this task?**

C. **Do you see any ways in which earlier life tasks affect their achievement of the task of intimacy?**

D. **What observations do not seem to fit with the above paragraphs on this stage of life? What ideas emerge from this?**

Generativity and Stagnation

As we transition from young adulthood to middle age we leave behind the prominent concerns of intimacy and isolation and move into the longest stage of all. It can start as early as age 30, is almost certainly in full swing by the time one is in one's forties and ends when a serious physical illness causes one to "retire," not just the career retirement as when we leave a job, but a broad spectrum retirement from the multifaceted concerns of the middle aged person. What are middle aged people concerned about? Haven't they "made it"? They have a career, a family, they know about intimate relationships; they are old, so they should feel confidence and trust and all the early developmental virtues, right? Well, yes, one would hope that the middle-aged person had achieved the previous life stages, and that this should free up much of their energy for those around them. Their sphere of concern enlarges to their extended family, their community, their neighborhood, their region, their nation, perhaps even the world. They become more concerned with the big picture, where the world is going. Aware that much or most of their life is over, and yet with plenty of energy and experience, they can turn their energies to what things they might leave behind them. They can become "keepers of the culture." They can help the younger generation, by becoming a mentor, a leader, a sponsor, and a teacher. They can lead by example, by living out their values and keeping their creativity alive. To the individual who is capable of living this fully in middle age, life truly can begin, or begin again, at forty, and the midlife crisis can be one of life's great and generous, "multiple second chances."

Clearly, however, not everyone is this fortunate. Earlier tasks may have been left chronically unresolved and cast a pall over midlife, which becomes contaminated with loneliness, hopelessness or despair. This individual may lapse into a "rut" and fall into the distortion of stagnation. Instead of using the powers that so often accrue to those in their middle age for the sustainment and enhancement of positive, life-affirming values, they become stagnant and negativistic. They "go through the motions," perhaps counting the days until retirement and envying the young and hopeful. They use their power simply for the sake of using it, just "throwing their weight around," perhaps becoming a petty tyrant at home or in the office. They succumb to the distortion of *authoritism*. This authoritism, like all of the other distortions, seems to serve as a consolation prize for the *virtue* of the era, which is *care,* care for future generations.

It is as if the middle-aged person longs to be needed, to be of use, especially to the younger generation. Not to be needed in this way is as painful to the mid-lifer as loneliness is to the young adult, or, say, inferiority to the grade schooler.

Activity 23:
Think about yourself, and your own middle years, as they were, are, or will be.

A.   *What are you doing in your midlife to keep it generative? (Remember this era of life might last more than forty years!)*

B.   *Describe someone you know who is living a middle age era that you find inspiring. What makes it so? Are they being generative?*

C.   *Describe someone whose middle years are not inspiring to you. (Do not mention their name or write any identifying information.) Are they "stagnant"? What has lead to them not living as fully as they might during this epoch of life?*

     What might help them "move ahead"?

Ego Integrity and Despair-Disgust

This is the last stage of life, old age. It is impossible to give an age when it starts. For some it might come quite early, perhaps even as early as one's fifties, even earlier in cultures and times when life expectancy might be about forty five years. Others however might continue to live the vigorous engaged lifestyle of the previous stage well into their eighties, or even nineties. At some point, however, it is time to "slow down," to disengage from the world and its challenges, to retire, not just from one's job, but from the many concerns of the middle aged person. A shift occurs from *care* to *wisdom*. Of course, we hope that the person still cares, but Erikson would argue that they care in a wiser way than before. The older person, for whom the next stage of life is death becomes interested in that which has always been true, the eternal verities, and seeks meaning in *wisdom*—perhaps through religion, through meditation, through philosophy, through reflection and reminiscence. These activities help the person make sense of their life, help put it together into a meaningful whole, to tell a good story, and the person achieves a sense of integration. They are "together," and out of this togetherness flows a sense of calm and fortitude, faith and hope that can be very helpful to younger generations—a positive picture indeed!

On the other hand, of course, not everyone is so fortunate. Some individuals fight the entry into this stage, will not step aside and let the younger generation take over the helm, so to speak, and this can make it very difficult for all those who are younger and are affected by this. Further, not everyone is capable of "putting him or herself together" in this graceful fashion. They perhaps have not achieved the life tasks of the previous stages—have not established a firm identity, are suffering from deep loneliness or feelings of inferiority or hopelessness. These individuals will fear death; will be disgusted at the sickness and the decline of their bodies that has "sidelined" them; will rage at their unfulfilled promise, fall into deep feelings of despair and remorse over a life unlived and, in bitterness, will pretend to have the wisdom of old age and enjoy the fruits thereof. They will engage in the distortion of *sapientism*—the pretence of wisdom where there is none. They become the "guru" who exploits their followers. The fake "holy man" who predates upon those who are younger who, with distortions of their own, are looking for a sense of "specialness," or power, or someone to idolize. These situations can wreak much havoc in a society (and today the havoc can be at a global level). We see here the extreme importance of paying close attention to and caring for the integrity and functionality of the family since it is predominantly in the family, as I argued at the outset, that these developmental tasks are accomplished.

Activity 24:
Think of a person you know (be careful to conceal their identity) who you believe is in the stage of ego integrity-despair.

a.   Does Erikson's theory seem to fit, or not? How?

b.   What is this person's role in the family?

c.   What contributions does this individual make to their family?

d. What awarenesses have emerged for you as you reflect on this individual and their family?

There we have it--life's course, according to Erik Erikson. Of course, this is not the whole story, just one thread through the infinite complexity of life. I present it here as a beginning, to help us chart the developmental tasks that are taking place in the crucible of the family. It is my hope that it has alerted you to the enormous complexity that lies before the would-be "family manager"; and we have only begun!

Other Developmental Lines

It would be remiss of me to move ahead without acknowledging a few of the multitude of other developmental lines the human being follows, or works on through the life course. To study all of these in depth would take, in itself several lifetimes, but let us take at least a glance at a few of them before we move on to examine the influence of culture on the family and development.

Separation and Individuation

This developmental line has to do with the developing sense the individual has of being a separate individual, of being their own person, with their own boundaries, space, projects, feelings, ideas, ideals and so on. Many of us take this for granted, but it is a developmental accomplishment of many years, probably it is a lifelong task. Even though we quickly become physically separate from our mothers, it takes much longer to develop a sense of psychological separation. Margaret Mahler has excellently documented this process and many clinicians (Bowen, Masterson) have shown how it can be applied to developmental psychotherapy.

Attachment-Empathy

I have already mentioned the importance of attachment as a family function. It is also related, I believe, to the development of empathy, of the capacity to be in tune with the feelings of others, to resonate with others and to know how they are feeling. This capacity develops out of a prolonged and secure set of attachments in the early years of life and, upon that base, it continues to develop over the life span. Clearly, it provides an important counterbalance to the previous developmental line, for while it is important for humans to feel separate and differentiated, it is also vital that they feel connected and emotionally, "in sync" with others.

Object Constancy

This developmental line is very much connected with the previous two, but it is so important in my mind that it deserves a separate mention. Object constancy refers to the capacity of the individual to evoke an image of their caretaker when they are not there, and to derive some sense of security from that evoked image. This capacity, which appears to solidify with humans around the third year of life is crucial for the process of separation-individuation, crucial in the individual being able to "do their own thing" and is essential in regulating all the ups and downs of moods we are subject to when we are out there in the world. This inner object, in some of its better forms can take on the shape of a "guardian angel" that can soothe and comfort us when we are under stress. Object constancy grows best in a matrix of secure attachment with the freedom to explore and return to a secure base. Failures in attaining object constancy might show up in difficulties in later life in being on one's own or leaving home.

Chums

Friends, and the capacity to form friendships, is another extremely important developmental line. Harry Stack Sullivan emphasized the importance in middle childhood (that is, between 8 to 10 years of age) of learning to love a special friend—to become "best friends" with someone. This serves many useful functions. It helps one establish a life of one's own, apart from the family, and thus fosters differentiation. It teaches much about empathy, love and intimacy, and these skills will carry forward in vital ways to the intimacy that is required in adulthood. It may also help heal trauma and provide emotionally corrective experiences for some of the shortcomings of one's family of origin. Disruptions in the formation of these friendships (and these can occur due to frequent moves, hostility of the family towards external ties, racism, illnesses, and a host of other reasons) can get in the way of this important life task, leaving the individual vulnerable in upcoming stages. This is a developmental line that is frequently overlooked and underestimated in both its pathogenic and curative force. Children's hearts can be broken, their worlds shattered and their development seriously derailed by disruptions along this line.

Integrating Sex and Intimacy

Once again this life task is well described by Harry Stack Sullivan. It arises with great urgency and prominence in adolescence, but remains as an important task throughout the lifespan. The groundwork for it is laid down in the early months and years of life. Before puberty, the child has, we hope, learned a great deal about emotional contact, about intimacy, and while much of that has been sensual, involving skin contact, feeding, caresses, gazing and so on, it has not been sexual in the "adult" sense of the term, involving sexual passion, sexual drives and orgasm. This changes after puberty, and the individual has (at least) these twin motivations to satisfy—the need for emotional contact and the need for sexual satisfaction. The issue lies in how to integrate the two. One option is to have sex without intimacy; another is to have intimacy without sex. In between lie all shadings and mixtures of the two, all the different social and psychological arrangements people make to meet these two needs. Often they are compartmentalized. For example, a man might have a wife with whom he has infrequent sex and little emotional contact; he may have a mistress and be emotionally close with a set of male friends. Sometimes individuals will seek all of the above in one special relationship— they see their spouse as friend, lover, confidante and erotic adventurer. Culture, too, will play an important role in what forms these integrations will take. These are however, very powerful and important motivations, often carrying extra meanings resulting from childhood experiences, and, again, individuals frequently work on their integration throughout their life course. Recall too, that all this psychosocial work is being carried out in and around the family.

Integrating Good and Bad

The psychoanalyst Melanie Klein refers to this developmental phase (this life task, as I am calling it here) as the "depressive position." In everyday language, it refers to the useful capacity to "take the rough with the smooth," to accept, without getting despondent, that "into every life a little rain must fall." These everyday aphorisms capture the resilient capacity some people have to bounce back from a disappointment or setback without feeling that everything has therefore become spoiled. "Good enough" is good enough. There is an ensuing sense of satisfaction (not complacency, for there is still work to be done) and a lack of envy of others who might be fortunate.

The individual who is capable of doing this (and again this is a lifelong task) has overcome to some extent the infantile tendency to split the world into "very good" (perfect) and "very bad" pieces. They do not have to believe that something is either all good or all bad. It could be a mixture and still be satisfactory. Klein argues that this capacity to integrate good and bad and not to oscillate wildly from one extreme to the other emerges very early in life—during the first few months, as the baby is making its first connections with its mother, father and the world. It is thus very tied up with Erikson's notions about basic trust—trust in oneself, others and the world.

Emotional Development

This developmental line is drawn from the theory of Kazimierz Dabrowski, who posited that there were five levels of development, and at the highest levels one finds values such as compassion, empathy, concern, self awareness, self direction and an increased capacity for emotional contact and growth. This developmental line involves *positive disintegration*—a sort of "falling to pieces" so that one can put oneself back together in a more complex fashion. At the lowest levels of development one finds a lack of self-awareness, a belief in brute force and dominance and lack of empathy.

An entire chapter of this book is devoted to Dabrowski's theory of Positive Disintegration and how it might illuminate family life.

Cognitive Development

This developmental line has to do with the growth of the capacity to think. Many theorists have put forward ideas on how these capacities develop and what kinds of environments support healthy growth. Jean Piaget, for example posits a theory where the child moves from *egocentric and concrete* modes of thinking towards *decentered and abstract* modes of thought.

Language and Symbols

This developmental line has to do with the development of the capacities for speech, writing and the manipulation of signs, symbols and signals. This, again, is an enormous field, and many thinkers have offered theories. Of particular interest to a number of psychologists recently is the manner in which the individual uses language and symbols to construct an image of the world, themselves and others. Also of concern to psychotherapists is the extent to which and ways in which these images are open to change, especially as it concerns the narratives or stories we build of ourselves and others.

The Transitional Space

This developmental line refers to the development, in the individual, of a capacity to participate in and contribute to the imaginary realm of human existence. In its earliest forms, this might involve a baby using a "transitional object" (a soft cuddly toy, for example) as an "imaginary companion" to comfort itself. Later on, it might show up in the form of imaginary companions, or fantasy play. Yet later, it will take the form of art, poetry, song, and film, and religion—culture in general. It is this capacity to participate, both as a producer and user, of these products, that gives people a sense of meaning, of worthwhileness, of community and belonging—important in ways far beyond "entertainment." D.W. Winnicott is the psychoanalytic theorist who initiated this idea in his last book, "Playing and Reality."

Activity 25:
Select one of the "developmental lines" described in this last section. Write one way in which a family might support the development of this line and one way in which the family might impede development along this line.

a.   Developmental Line:

b.   One way in which a family might help development along this line.

c.   One way in which a family might hinder development along this developmental line.

I hope this section leaves you with the feeling that there is much yet to be learned in this domain—developmental life tasks and the family. At the same time, I hope that it has given you some ideas and some inroads into this domain, for it is a region that is of crucial importance for human well-being.

In the next section, we will broaden our scope. The family exists in a context, and this context has a culture that is extremely powerful in the way in which it shapes behavior inside the family. If we are to understand families, we must examine the forces culture exerts upon families and ways in which families react to these messages.

CHAPTER 3
Cultural Factors And The Family

In this chapter we will examine culture and its effects on family life. Families exist in communities, communities in regions, regions in nations, and nations in civilizations. At each of these levels, we find sets of group beliefs about behavior that are very powerful and impinge upon the process and structure of the family. We start with a summary and then go, step by step through a more detailed account of thirty dimensions of culture and how each dimension can affect the family we live in.

Summary

Thirty Dimensions of Culture
The following is a briefly annotated list of thirty cultural dimensions that I have found to be worth consideration in various contexts—teaching, counseling, research, supervision, and families. I find this "dimensional" approach to cultural sensitivity more flexible and robust than the often-used "categorical" approach where individuals are placed in categories (for example, "white," "African American," "Asian") that usually are ill fitting and often experienced as a negation. The dimensional approach enables the person to locate him or herself in an "n-space" that is unique to them and that is dynamic, paying heed to the notion that culture is constantly in a state of flux.

I believe that this dimensional approach also pays more respect to the inherent holism in cultures, namely that one element of a culture is, to a greater or lesser extent, related to all other elements of a culture. You change one element or dimension, and everything else is affected.

The list is not in any particular order, but can be understood as a sort of "check list" to go through when attempting to understand any given cultural situation.

Culture is here defined along the standard anthropological lines of "ideas and beliefs about behavior that have been learned and are shared by a group."

1. Familism: the degree to which the culture places a value on membership in an integrated family, however the family might be defined in that culture.

2. Authority: the manner in which authority is gained and maintained in that culture and attitudes towards authority.

3. Formality: the degree of formality versus informality in the culture—casualness versus strict guidelines for behavior.

4. Which "Wave" (as described by Alvin Toffler in his book, "The Third Wave") is culture in? Is the culture transitioning from one wave to the next?

5. What is the household/kinship structure in this culture? What is a family? What is a "normal" living arrangement?

6. Marriage/divorce: What are the patterns and attitudes towards these?

7. Social control: What are the means used? e.g., Is adjudication or mediation used? Are there multiple systems of social control?

8. Intensity: What is the emotional tone and energy level in this culture? Is it intense, like the Yanomamo, of the Brazilian rain forest, or low key, like the Dani, of Irian Jaya?

9. Attitudes towards sex: Where does this culture stand on the dimension of sex positive-sex negative attitudes?

10. Core values: What are the core values for this culture? Ferociousness, honor, intellect, achievement, endurance?

11. What is the place of magic, religion and science in this culture?

12. Attitudes towards children: Are children seen as little adults? Extensions of parents? Loved? Treated with indifference?

13. Ethnic history: What is the history of this culture? How powerful is it? Does it interact with individual history in potent ways? (See Erikson, 1963)

14. Processes of change: How much is this culture changing? In what ways?

15. Aging: How are the old treated?

16. Death and Dying: What are the attitudes toward this? What structures are available to cope with this in this culture?

17. Rituals: What are the key rituals or *"rites de passage"* in this culture? What do they tell us about this culture?

18. Aesthetics: What are the aesthetic values of this culture? What is the place of aesthetics in this culture?

19. Time: How is time structured in this culture? What are the cultural attitudes towards time?

20. Historical events and eras: What were key historical events and eras in this culture that affected cohorts of this culture in different ways, for example, the Vietnam War, World War Two, and The Great Depression?

21. Political institutions: What are the vital political institutions in this culture—how are big decisions made? Parliament, "big men," priests? How is access gained to political power?

22. Gender: How is gender socially constructed in this culture? What are the assigned roles of men and women?

23. What is the overall degree of enculturation? Are members of this culture aware of other cultures? Are they cosmopolitan?

24. Class structure: What is the class structure in this society? What are its markers? Is it open and obvious or disguised? Is there mobility?

25. Reality: What is regarded as "reality" in this culture? What is regarded as "common sense" and what is seen as unreal, fantastic, and crazy?

26. Work and patterns of economic activity: What are the patterns of production? How do people make livings? Complex or simple? Are there rhythms or cycles? What kind of work is it? Is it risky work? What demands are made? What is the "work ethic"?

27. Individualism-Communitarianism: to what extent is individual behavior regulated by expectations of the community? Is it a "do your own thing" culture, or a "consider others before you act" kind of culture?

28. Race: The social construction of physical differences. How is race socially constructed? What meanings does the concept of race carry?

29. Love: Attitudes towards forms of love, for example, romantic, companionate, passionate, courtly love. What are regarded as "ideal" forms of love?

30. The Body: Cultural attitudes towards the human body. Is the body regarded as being separate from the mind? Is it something to be mastered? Is it used as a vehicle for status? How?

Families exist in cultures. It makes a big difference whether your family is located in rural France or on the South Side of Chicago. Your neighborhood, community, region, nation, even civilization, will affect the dynamics of your family.

"Culture" is a very complex concept. Here it is defined as the set of beliefs about behavior that is learned and shared by a group. These ideas and beliefs can be envisaged as being directed at the family, at guiding its dynamics and function. It is almost as if cultural messages are sent to the family, especially the parents, who then base their decisions on this received culture. Much of the time this is unconscious, for most of culture is "taken as read," as common sense, as reality.

Culture, however, is not always received uncritically. Families, for a variety of reasons, will sometimes make a stand and resist certain cultural expectations, not infrequently trying to bring about a change in the culture through persuasive or political activity. Parents who decide to "home school" their children or who resist their children's pleas to purchase only expensive brand-name sneakers and clothes may be examples of this. Culture is a very important, but often underestimated, driver of behavior.

In the following section, we will examine 30 dimensions of culture and give an example of how each dimension of culture might affect family life. At the end you should have an idea (perhaps dizzying) of the complexity of culture and the multiple and complex ways in which families can be affected by cultural forces. The list is in no particular order. Bear in mind that the field is rendered even more complex by virtue of the fact that these dimensions operate not only on their own but in combinations, exerting even more variegated effects.

Familism

Familism concerns the extent to which the culture is family-oriented--the extent to which it is felt that family members should stick together in a cohesive way.

Like all the other variables here, "familism" is very complex. It has to do with cohesion--the extent to which the family stays together spatially. Some cultures expect its members to leave, to migrate, to go away to school. In others this would be uncommon.

Sometimes family culture is about cohesion in an ideological sense. For example, it might be expected in a culture that all members of the family share the same beliefs, while in others "family non-conformity" might be expected.

In some cultures "family name," "family pride" and family-based identity are important. Sometimes this can extend to the notion of a clan--a group of related families. In such cultures a person might feel a sense of pride or shame based on the behavior of other family members. At the other extreme, in low family-pride-driven cultures, individuals' pride and self-esteem will be little affected by the accomplishments or transgressions of their relatives.

The dimension of familism is very complex and has obvious impacts on family dynamics. It can be regarded as an admixture of seven sub-dimensions. Broadly, "familism" has to do with the extent to which the family believes in togetherness and in having a cohesive identity. Some cultures press for a high degree of familism, while others do not.

This dimension of familism can seen as a compilation of six sub-dimensions:
  a. spatial cohesion
  b. mutual indebtedness
  c. family pride--family name
  d. warmth
  e. material support
  f. attitudinal cohesion

a. Spatial Cohesion

Cultures vary in the extent to which there is an assumption that the family should "stick together" spatially. In some cultures it is expected that members will move away, while in others, to move away from one's family constitutes a major transgression of a cultural norm.

England, during its imperial era, required many of its citizens to relocate to far-flung corners of the empire to administer its possessions. Thus, low spatial cohesion was accepted as a way of life. People moved away a lot. Children were introduced to these experiences early; often the middle-class children would be sent to distant boarding schools, where they would live, from the age of seven to eighteen. Such separations would be unthinkable in other high familism cultures, such as many peasant farming communities, but where empire has to be served, one where allegiance to the state is required or where the machinery of production requires a mobile workforce, such a form of low family cohesion will be common. This brings with it a wide array of other effects on people and on society. Several of the functions of family life (mentioned in Chapter 1) will perhaps be compromised or, at best, have to be picked up by other social agencies--the school, state or church.

b. Mutual Indebtedness

In some cultures, families are bound together by beliefs regarding mutual indebtedness. This indebtedness may be material in the form of gifts with strings attached, favors that must be returned. For example, a father who keeps his daughter "bound" by a substantial trust fund upon which she has come to rely but which she fears losing, should the father look upon her with disfavor. Or perhaps the parents buy their newly-married son or daughter a house nearby, thereby assuring spatial cohesion, and, perhaps, conformity.

At other times the sense of indebtedness is more abstract or emotional. For example, parents might emphasize the sacrifices they have made for their children with the implicit or explicit expectation that the children pay them back. Children in such a situation may feel that if they move away or "buck the system," they are betraying their parents.

In another culture this sense of "owing" is low and the children feel free to leave or be different without a incurring a deep sense of betrayal.

c. Family Pride

Some cultures are more heavily based on family pride or family name, perhaps even connecting this family name to a clan-name, a group of families. Thus, one will find in these cultures an increased familism as people say sentences beginning with, "We Dangerfields..." or asking questions like, "Are they the Blythes of Boston...?" The notion of dynasty is connected with this concept and shows up in aristocratic sub-cultures or in industrial, capitalistic, political or intellectual multigenerational dynasties such as the Kennedys, the Rockefellers, the Stuarts, and so on. In these subcultures the behavior of one family member can reflect upon and affect everyone else in the family in dramatic ways. In other cultures "family name" is relatively inconsequential and familism is similarly reduced. In such a family, there would be little interest in a "family crest" or even, perhaps, in the family lineage and evolving identity over the years.

d. Warmth

Research into families has shown that this is a very important dimension of family life. It is also a feature of cultures. While it is difficult to capture or measure underlying warmth, overt displays of warmth are quite easily picked up on. Cultures vary in the amount of hugging, kissing, smiling, personal space, caressing, stroking, touching and eye contact allowed or regarded as normal. In some cultures children routinely sleep with their parents, while in others they are required to sleep separately, perhaps even in another room. Tones of voice range from cold to warm, and these, too, are affected by cultural messages.

Thus, high degrees of familism might be driven by high degrees of cultural warmth, encouraging cohesion. By contrast, in "cooler" cultures, familism might be reduced.

e. Material Support

Some families, in some cultures, are held together by the material support they offer one another. This material support is offered relatively freely, thus differentiating itself from the previously-mentioned feature of mutual indebtedness. For example, in some cultures it is expected that everyone will pitch in at harvest time, or that all will contribute to a child's college fund or help a relative through a period of unemployment. Funds may be given to help in migration to improve the economic well-being of an individual family member.

f. Attitudinal Cohesion

Some cultures, and some families operating in those cultures, operate under the aegis of an expectation of attitudinal conformity. Thus, family members are expected to conform, to go with the flow. In these families and cultures, "being a black sheep," not fitting in, could be very socially costly, perhaps even physically dangerous. In another culture, non-conformity might be par for the course and, by extension, not viewed as unusual in a family. Cohesion, with regard to all in the family having the same attitudes (values, politics, religion, beliefs, lifestyle, etc.), is reduced, as is this form of familism.

Familism is a very complex feature of culture which has enormous power over family life. As we shall see, it also interacts with all the other domains of cultural and family life.

Activity 26:
Think of your family or a family you know. To what extent and in what ways is this family operating on assumptions of spatial cohesiveness? Is it assumed the family will live nearby, or is it accepted that family members will move away? What effects do these assumptions seem to have on the rest of the family?

Now do the same assessment for each of the remaining five dimensions of familism.
b)   Mutual Indebtedness

c)   Family Pride - Family Name

d)   *Warmth*

e)   *Material Support*

f.   *Attitudinal Cohesion*

Attitudes toward Children

Cultures vary in complex ways in their attitudes toward children. In some cultures children are prized, in others romanticized. In other cultures they are treated with hostility, or abandoned. In some cultures they are treated as little adults from early on, while in others they are treated as small beings, very different from adults, living in their own different world. In some cultures the child is regarded as a possession by the parents, while in other cultures the parents are encouraged in various ways to give up this possession of the child. To further complicate this, we must recall that these attitudes will vary greatly by gender. Attitudes and expectations will differ between boys and girls. These attitudes, in all their complexity, will have effects on the family. What is expected of children? When to do they become responsible? What is "normal" for a child? How should they be brought up?

Activity 27:
Think of your culture. What are prevailing attitudes toward children? How did this show up in your family or a family you are familiar with?

Authority

Cultural assumptions regarding authority vary greatly. In some cultures authority or power is "softened" as with a velvet glove. Brute displays of power are shunned and there is an attempt at a negotiated settlement. Many "liberal" middle-class families of Europe and the United States might fit this stereotype. In other cultures more autocratic manifestations of power are expected and this cultural belief manifests itself in the way decisions are made in the family where power might be centralized and unquestioned.

Linked to this are different cultural assumptions regarding motivation, learning behavior change and punishment. Similarly, these will "work their way into" the culture of the family, at times dramatically affecting the process and outcomes.

Patterns of authority have also been shown to be related to class and the type of work one does, each of these being associated with sub cultural experiences. Workers on production lines are more likely to exist in an autocratic environment than, say, those in the professional classes. Here we ask," Who is in charge of what in this family, and how do they obtain and maintain this authority?"

Activity 28:
What are the expectations with regard to authority in a culture in which you participate? In what ways does it affect your family?

Attitudes toward Sex

Like all the other dimensions we are examining here, attitude toward sex is a complex composite dimension. One element of this dimension is the extent to which a culture is "sex positive" or "sex negative." Sex positive cultures like sex and approve of it as an activity. While there will be rules governing certain aspects of sexual life (where, when, with whom, how), in general the attitude is that sex is something to be enjoyed. Sex may be enjoyed recreationally and is not only for procreation.

Sex negative cultures are suspicious of sex. It is avoided and often regarded as sinful or immoral. It is often seen as a necessary evil for procreation. The sex act itself is often kept as brief as is necessary, and might often be done with coverings or clothing to prevent too much exposure. Sexual pleasure has often to be "paid for" with shame and guilt.

Clearly such cultural features will have powerful impacts on family life. Families are charged with the task of socializing children into the sexual ways of their society. Children will observe parents' sexual behavior as governed by cultural norms. It is likely that aspects of family warmth are affected by these cultural assumptions. But it is far more complex than even this.

For example, cultures can yoke sexuality to religion. Sexuality may become a form of worship. Sexuality may, on the other hand, be seen as profane. In addition, cultural attitudes toward sexual technologies vary. Contraceptive technologies are very available in some cultures while in others they are forbidden.

These factors all impact family dynamics. To add to the complexity, cultures are often not uniform--the culture of the neighborhood can be different from the culture of the school, college or factory. Furthermore, culture is in a constant state of flux.

Frequently the topics of adolescent sexuality and sexual education are "hotspots" at which the underlying cultural assumptions regarding sex can be observed.

Activity 29:
Characterize the attitudes toward sex in a culture with which you are familiar. Show how these cultural attitudes may have affected family life.

Magic, Religion and Science

Bronislaw Malinowski was one of the first anthropologists to codify the relationship between these three domains and culture. Simplified, his argument was that when groups face reasonably predictable and safe environments, they tend to gain control, guide behavior, and predict the future using science. As the situation and the task becomes more complex and risky (as, say, fishermen leave the security of the lagoon and operate in tricky offshore waters), so they turn to magic as a way of predicting and controlling--perhaps using amulets, charms or chants. As the situation becomes very dangerous, risky and unpredictable, so the group shifts to the techniques of religion, using prayer and invoking the power of a god, or multiple gods. As the old saying goes, "There are no atheists in foxholes." When our lives are threatened, we often turn to a superhuman power for help.

Western civilization, over the past few centuries, has placed the scientific approach in a very privileged position, and magic and religion, on the whole, have retreated as science and technology have gained in their power. Many cultures have not so completely fallen under the hegemony of science and technology. In these cultures the power of magic and religion are still considerable.

Families thus can exist in cultures that rely more on science, magic or religion as explanatory modes. Families will also have internal cultures that vary along these dimensions.

In some families this internal culture will be relatively congruent with the surrounding culture, whereas with other families there will be a difference between the culture of the family and that of its surround. This may show up when the child encounters different modes of explanation in school, family, church and community.

Not infrequently in immigrant communities, in "westernized" societies, the parents bring with them a magic and religion-based explanatory system while their children, growing up in a "Western" cultural matrix, use more "science" in their thinking. This, in turn, creates intra-familial tensions. Even in the absence of migration, historical trends involving the decline of magic and religion and the ascent of science can result in intergenerational tensions.

Activity 30:

Think of a family and its members. Think of the extent to which they rely on magic, religion or science to explain everyday life and its occurrences.

a. Are there differences between the generations along these lines? How?

b. Are there differences between the family and its surrounding culture along these lines? How?

Core Values

Cultures organize themselves around core values—things like achievement, fair play, ferociousness, intellectual acumen, hard work, honor, risk-taking, kindness, and so on. Often these values are different not only for cultures or subcultures, but also for genders and age groups within a culture.

Families operate within this cultural values matrix and are profoundly affected by it. Often, what is important in the culture becomes important in the family--being a success, becoming wealthy, being reliable, and being obedient. Tensions in families can often be understood as resulting from family members having different "readings" and different renditions of what is important in their culture, what is important in life.

Activity 31:
Write out a list of what you perceive to be the core values of your culture or subculture.

a. How do items on this list affect your family?

b. Does everybody in your family have the same perception of cultural core values? What impact does this have on family dynamics?

Attitudes and Assumptions about Children

What people believe about children varies in very complex ways from culture to culture. So complex is this variation that, as elsewhere in this section, only certain aspects will be touched on here.

Some cultures have positive attitudes and beliefs toward children while others do not. In some cultures children are viewed somewhat romantically or even mystically, while in others they might be viewed quite pragmatically, perhaps as another mouth to feed or as a potential source of labor.

Significantly, some cultures assume that children, from quite early on, are like small adults and treat them as such. In other cultures childhood is seen as a separate preserve, children being regarded as special and different beings with their own way of seeing and thinking, requiring, therefore, special different treatment.

Clearly, this is just a beginning list of many different ways cultures can orient themselves toward children. Clearly, too, these attitudes will have very powerful effects on family life. Answers to questions such as, "What are children like?," "What developmental stages do they go through, and when?," "What should they be told?," "How should they be disciplined?," "How much influence should they have?," will all be affected by such cultural belief systems.

Activity 32:
Cultural assumptions regarding children change over time. Interview an older person, asking them how, in their perception, attitudes toward children have changed through time. Write down three differences you discover.

    1.

    2.

    3.

Now write your reaction to these perceptions of your interviewee.

Attitudes toward Death

Again, we find this category contains complexity--a complexity I compress here for convenience. And, again, cultural attitudes toward death and dying and the rituals and social activities that are related to these attitudes have enormous impacts on families.

For example, some cultures are, to use the phrase of Elizabeth Kübler-Ross, "death denying." These cultures prefer to act as though death did not exist. They are averse to talking about death, will use euphemisms for death (for example, "passing over," "going over the great divide") and avoid the dying and the dead. It could be argued that in these cultures, the grieving process is suppressed or repressed in families, making it far more difficult to work through the mourning process described by Freud. In other cultures that are not so death denying, death is more out in the open, more discussable and, hence, families suffering loss have more social opportunities for "working through" their grief to a resolution, what Kübler-Ross calls, "acceptance."

In the movie *Ordinary People*, for example, the family is dealing with the loss of the son, Buck, in a death-denying cultural matrix, and this is one of the several factors straining their attempts to cope.

Activity 33:
Think of your culture along the dimension of "death denying" versus "death accepting." Where does it stand? What evidence do you have to support your assessment?

In what ways is this reflected in family life in your culture?

Do these effects on the family appear to be functional or not, helpful or hindering? How?

Attitudes toward Aging and the Aged

Cultures vary in their attitudes toward their old members. In some cultures we find a reverence for the aged. Perhaps the aged occupy positions of power and prestige. They may be regarded as being wise or as having useful experience, making them valuable members of society.

In other cultures the aged are regarded as a non-productive liability. Negative ageism may characterize them as slow, resistant to change or even as learning-disabled. In cultures such as this, the old will often be excluded from much of social life, perhaps kept in concentrations in institutions such as nursing homes.

This factor will have a strong impact on family life. People age in families. How they are treated and consequent family dynamics will be very much affected by the expectations and beliefs in the cultural surround.

This effect will be especially notable where there is a discontinuity or conflict between the internal family cultures. For example, if the culture-at-large does not revere and positively value the aged, but the "culture carriers" in the family (usually the parents) do, then many of the family's internal arrangements organized around their old members will be seen as irrational. When, for example, a son or a daughter takes time off or asks for a readjustment in their work schedule so that they may care for an aging parent, this may not be understood by their boss, colleagues or professors.

Activity 34:
Think of your culture. What are its attitudes toward the old?

What are two consequences of these beliefs and attitudes on family life?

How do you feel personally about the attitudes you describe above?

Intensity and Display Rules

This, again, is a global composite dimension. Broadly, some cultures value intensity in all, many or some domains, while others are low-keyed--emotionally, spiritually, intellectually and physically. In some cultures it is further complicated by *rules of display*. For example, in much of English culture it might be acceptable to feel quite intensely, but not *de rigueur* to display such intense feelings in public, in undisguised, "uncoded" form.

In other cultures excitability, intensity and displays of same are quite the norm. A visitor to this culture may feel a fight is about to break out when all that is happening is a sharing of ideas.

Cultural rules regarding intensity and its display will have an impact on family life, since it will regulate passions and their expression in the family. In the movie, *Ordinary People*, for example, the culture of upper middle class whites contributes to the restriction of emotional expression in the family, making it very difficult for them to make emotional contact and deal with their loss.

Many movies pick up on this theme when dealing, often humorously, with inter-cultural pairings. In *My Big Fat Greek Wedding*, we see an open, vigorous expression of emotion in the Greek family contrasted with the prim and proper "Anglos." Woody Allen, in *Annie Hall*, exploits similar differences between his Jewish family and Annie's "Nordic-seeming" background. In addition, many students from the United States of America are surprised at the low-keyedness of the couple in Ingmar Bergman's, "Scenes from a Marriage" as they discuss the husband's affair.

Activity 35:
Compare two families you know. Do they have different rules and expectations regarding intensity and display? How do these differences or similarities shown?

To what extent do these families' similarities and differences regarding intensity and display reflect cultural differences?

Ethnic History

Many cultural variables are affected by narratives of ethnic history, of the story, or stories of my people. These narratives are told and retold in different forms and through different media, usually by the old to the young. In the telling, much is communicated, much is transmitted--core values, desirable traits, ideas of identity, core concepts, and hopes for the future. These narratives work their way into the personality of the individual. Families celebrate holidays organized around these historical narratives. Often these narratives are re-told in the family at this time. Thus, an English family might be influenced by narratives of King Arthur or Saint George; Mexican families by narratives of Benito Juarez or Montezuma; and African American families by narratives of Dr. Martin Luther King or Frederick Douglas.

In broader culture there may be competition between narratives as a result of differential deployments of power. Certain narratives of certain cultural groups may be suppressed or repressed so as to preserve vested interests in power dynamics. Thus, many families may find themselves cut off from the narratives of their cultural history. Given the powerful organizing power of these narratives, this will usually have detrimental effects on the family. An example of this might be the oft-undertold narratives of the indigenous peoples of America (especially in the United States). Despite recent gains in this area, much still remains to be done.

Activity 36:
Think of your family or a family you know. Briefly write out one of the historical stories from the culture of this family.

Now analyze this narrative:
c.   *What values are reflected in this story?*

d.   *What does this story say about the relationship of the individual to the community?*

e.   *What sorts of behavior are regarded as undesirable in this narrative?*

f.   *How do these factors seem to affect the family in question?*

Class Structure

Societies, even wealthy ones, where the process of "embourgeoisement" (the process of increasing the size of the middle class) has proceeded apace, have class structures. Families in this class system are affected by and have to negotiate tensions arising from social class.

These tensions take many different forms and they can affect family dynamics in very powerful ways. For example, much film and literature documents family tensions that arise when a member of a working class family has "middle class" aspirations. D.H. Lawrence's *Sons and Lovers* and the movie, *Billy Elliott,* examine this theme. Even *Madame Bovary* can be read from a class dynamics perspective as the forlorn heroine strives for a cosmopolitan, romantic, upper middle class life in middle class provincial France.

Sometimes parents attempt to live in a neighborhood that is above their class, or at least, above their income. Sometimes the children of these parents feel chronically left out at school, only to have their friends from "the wrong side of the tracks" disparaged and rejected by their parents. Again, these children may be witness to chronic financial strain and anxiety over how they look to the neighbors.

Sometimes the story is told in reverse. Parents might elect to live in a neighborhood that is socially and financially a notch or two below their status. While these families may be more financially relaxed in the neighborhood, the children may be labeled as "rich" or "snooty" and may suffer as a consequence.

Some families, having just "arrived," say, in the middle class, may be anxious about an all-too-easy slide back into the lower classes. Such families--in an anxious effort to keep up, not slip back or not to lose face--can become very rigid and controlling of one another, very concerned over how they might look. This can seriously limit emotional expression and spontaneity in the family.

Social class interacts with all the other variables in this section. Frequently, the upper middle class cultures have norms restricting expression of emotion or intensity of any kind, while all classes have norms restricting language use and expression of sexuality.

Marriages can be intercultural insofar as they occur between partners of different classes. There is a widespread tendency for men to "marry down" (i.e., to marry a woman who is younger, poorer and of lower social status) and this is widely distributed in cultural narratives, for example the plays, stories and movies of: *Pygmalion, Maid in Manhattan, Pretty Woman, My Fair Lady,* even (with tragic consequences) *Carmen* and *Carmen Jones.*

This section could become a book. Suffice it to say, if one wishes to understand a family, one should ask questions about class--the ideas regarding class in the family, the "class history" and "class myths" of the family (often these show up as political narratives and reminiscences), along with class perceptions and aspirations. An important "angle" will be gained on the tensions and dynamics of family life.

In a family I once knew, the father would often tell how, when he was a young man, an upper class man had asked him to hold his horse in a disrespectful way. The father would tell how he had told the man, using colorful, working class language that he would not be ordered around by a "toffee-nosed twit." This story seemed to form part of the organization of the culture of the family—a culture of robust, direct speaking, lower class individuals, who were not subservient to the upper classes. As the family got wealthier and some of the children went to college, it became more "middle class" and had, in fact, to rub shoulders with the erstwhile despised upper classes. This created tensions in the family at a systemic and individual level.

Activity 37:
Reflect on social class and how it affects your family or a family you are familiar with. Write down one story about this family that has to do with social class.

Now write the lesson imparted by the story. What is the moral of the story? How does this moral show up in this family? For example, does it serve to increase family cohesion, to control behavior or to instill values?

Gender

Cultures vary greatly in the ways in which they think about gender. They vary in the number of genders that are thought to exist and the extent to which one is "stuck" in a gender, or how much one can, temporarily or permanently, change gender.

Societies also vary in the behavior that is expected of the different genders and in, for example, how girls and boys, men and women are supposed to behave. They vary in their accepted "signposts" of gender.

These cultural expectations come right into the family, affecting its task of socialization. Different expectations, different concerns are held for boys and girls, and they are pulled, willy-nilly, into roles, roles that may or may not fit the emerging personality of the child or the ideology of the parents or community. In some "traditional" cultures, for example, girls are expected to do housework and child care from, say, seven or eight years on while boys are free to play or, perhaps, study. In other cultures this division of labor might be vigorously challenged. In yet other cultures and families, there might be uncertainty and confusion as to the roles and behavior that are appropriate for boys and girls.

Again, this domain interacts with other domains. For example, different rules regarding emotions, intensity, display, authority, and so on are frequently held for boys and girls, and, again, these change with age. For example, old women might be permitted, for example, to behave in a managerial, authoritative way while young girls are expected to be shy, retiring and submissive.

Perhaps overt sexuality is permitted for young men but not for older men or women. Such cultural rules can indeed be dizzyingly complex (and also in a state of change). Families, often attempting to mirror their surrounding culture, can mirror this dynamic complexity.

Activity 38:
What culturally-driven gender differences do you notice in a family with which you are familiar?

What effects does this have on the family?

Historical Events and Eras

Historical events and eras such as 9/11, the Vietnam War, and the Great Depression impact cultures in powerful ways, changing moods, values and norms. Families exist in cultures differentially affected by these events. Families are also comprised of individuals who carry within themselves the impress of these transformative cultural experiences.

Thus, grandparents, who recall the Great Depression, may save paper bags, newspapers and lengths of thread and may "eat anything," while their "Baby Boomer" offspring consume and waste with abandon, mistrust authority and "manage their stress."

In multicultural families, historical events from across the globe can be brought into contact over the kitchen table. Thus, the Chinese "Cultural Revolution," the regime of Pol Pot, Paris in May 1968, Argentina during the 1970s--all these can meet in families, especially in the mobile mix of the global village.

Activity 39:
What were some of the historical events that affected members of your family or a family you know, both immediate and extended?

Write down several ways these historical events may have affected your family.

Rituals

Cultures have a variety of rituals that serve many functions. On the surface they are celebrations, markers of respect, or "milestones" demarcating life changes. Unconsciously, they may serve to increase solidarity, raise morale, protect against anxiety, depression or fear, or help maintain a sense of control.

Families frequently participate in rituals, more so if it exists in a culture that is dense in rituals. These rituals can have a wide array of effects on families. Sometimes they consume much of the families' resources: time, money, food, and goods. Sometimes they serve very functional ends for the family: making contacts, linking to resources, providing support and emotional contact, and fostering socialization of the young. Sometimes, however, these rituals consume much energy, and alienate the family as a whole, or members of the family.

Rituals can be regarded as being like social neurotic symptoms. They represent a group's compromise solution to an intractable problem that the group has long since repressed. Just as such symptoms in an individual can enable them to function in a specific realm (as when, for example, a good luck charm enables a batter to function better in a baseball diamond), so a social ritual can enable functioning in a given realm (as when a wedding shower helps newlyweds establish a new home and helps protect them from the envy of the community in with they live).

The parallel can be extended such that just as with individuals, rituals can hypertrophy and impede functioning (as is the case where obsessive "undoing" prevents the completion of a task). So, a family or community can have its functioning damaged by the too vigorous observation of a ritual (as is the case when a family might impoverish itself in the staging of a young daughter's "coming out" party or cotillion).

Alternatively, some families suffer from a lack of rituals and the benefits they can offer. The family might find it hard to come together for celebrations or rituals that might help the family perform its tasks and its members cope.

118

Activity 40:
Write three paragraphs of "free writing" (i.e. writing the first things that come into your head) on the rituals in your family or a family you know.

Now reflect on this free writing. Write down one awareness arising from this exercise.

Waves

Alvin Toffler, in *The Third Wave*, shows how families vary in structure depending on the stage of technology in the surrounding society. The technology, be it "First Wave" (agricultural), "Second Wave" (industrial), or Third Wave (post-industrial), affects everything, culture and family included. Broadly, Toffler argues that the First Wave family is extended and multigenerational. The Second Wave family tends to be nuclear and two generational (parents and children). And, the Third Wave involves a smorgasbord of family structures, including the foregoing structures and single parent, homosexual and commune-style families.

Although there is much to question in Toffler's formulations, this model does provide us with ideas that sensitize as to influence of technology, culture and family.

Activity 41 :
Think of a family, perhaps even a fictional family that is clearly in a different wave from the one you live in. How is it similar?

How is it different?

Household - Extent and Structure

It is a good idea when thinking about a family to ask the question, "What is the typical form of a household in this culture?" For example, while in some cultures it is usual for the family unit to consist of only parents and children, in other cultures it may be expected for a married couple to move in with the mother of the groom. Similarly, in some cultures it is assumed that children live with their parents, while with others this might not be the case. There might, for example, be quite a free movement of children amongst relatives or clan members.

Cultures have widely varying assumptions regarding living arrangements. In some cultures older members are expected to live in the house and be cared for. In others they are expected to live separately in retirement or nursing homes.

Frequently, in conditions of poverty, people will form extended families. Perhaps the famous "nuclear family" is even a status symbol standing for membership in the middle classes, betokening, as it does, a capacity to survive on one income. (Although nowadays in the United States of America, both parents have frequently to work in order to sustain the lifestyle they would like.)

Activity 42:
How has the household (i.e. the number of people living under one roof) of your family or a family you know changed over the years?

What factors lead to these changes?

What were the advantages and disadvantages of these changes in household size and structure?

Marriage and Divorce

Cultures vary in their beliefs and laws regarding who may get married and when and what feelings or sentiments should accompany marriage. They also vary in the ways in which they regulate divorce--Is it allowed? For whom? Is it "respectable"? What constitutes grounds for divorce? How easy or difficult is it to obtain a divorce?

These assumptions will have enormous impact on the shape and feel of families--whether families stick together unhappily because cultural and legal forces keep them so; whether families break up and re-form with new members because the culture enables divorce and remarriage--all this will have tremendous impact on, for example, children growing up in a family with a "loveless marriage" or having spent much of their childhood in a series of different family arrangements.

In the United States, at the beginning of the 21st century, the question is being broached as to whether homosexual marriage should be legally recognized. The culture, along with the legal system, is in a state of flux. This very flux, the very question itself, implies a cultural shift.

Activity 43:
Think of a culture you are familiar with. Respond to the following.

a) How important is it that people in this culture marry for love? What are some impacts of these beliefs?

b) What are attitudes toward divorce? What seem to be the impacts of these attitudes?

c) Do these attitudes (discussed above) seem to be changing? How? What effects are these changes having?

Social Control

Again, this is a very large and complex domain. Social control has to do with the ways in which deemed misbehavior or improper behavior is dealt with. It also has to do with how conflict is resolved. Social control can be informal, as in when a friend or an elder is called in to resolve a dispute, or it can be formal, as when, say, a police officer is brought in to resolve a domestic fight. Cultures have different views on whether it is appropriate to react to a conflict situation using formal or informal techniques.

In some cultures regulatory agents, departments of family and children's concerns, are routinely called upon to affect family issues in formal, legalistic ways, while in other cultures, this is unheard of; issues such as these would be dealt with (or not) informally.

Cultures also have varying levels of trust for formal and informal systems. Subcultures may be very informally regulated and members might feel threatened or unsure of the formal (say legal) system. Similarly, members of formally regulated cultures may feel all at sea, and lacking in the "street smarts" of the informal system.

Families operate in this cultural matrix, often having to learn different ways of operating when they change, say, locations or class. Furthermore, members of the same family may bring with them experiences from different cultures and different degrees of informality and formality.

A further dimension of interest involves access to political power, be it formal or informal. Some families operate in such a way and in such a culture that they feel politically empowered. They can get help from a lawyer, alderman, chief, lieutenant, ward boss, mayor or community leader. Other families feel cut adrift, disenfranchised, lacking such linkages, existing or potential to political power.

This could have powerful influences on the internal dynamics of the family. Feelings of helplessness are linked to depression. A feeling of efficacy fosters ambition and hopefulness. These feelings and others will profoundly affect the texture of the family.

Activity 44:
Give an example of an informal control that operates in your community that affects your family.

What is the impact of this on your family?

Processes of Change

Cultures are never static. They are always changing. Technology changes and affects culture. Science opens up and closes possibilities and affects culture. People move, or are moved; wars are fought, won and lost; companies implode and expand globally. All these change culture--sometimes rapidly, sometimes slowly.

Families operating in stable, unchanging cultural surrounds will perhaps operate with a stronger sense of tradition. There may be greater continuity and similarity of cultural values between the generations. As the process of cultural change speeds up, so the younger generations of the family start to confront different realities from the older generation and the generation gap ensues.

Arguably, if cultural change reaches very high rates, all generations confront change relatively equally and perhaps this "gap" is reduced. The old as well as the young face cultural uncertainty. (Perhaps this is part of the postmodern condition.)

Studies of societies undergoing cultural change indicate that those groups most involved in the transition experience the highest levels of anxiety. "Traditionals" and "avant-gardists," that is, those who have either not changed and those who have fully accepted the change, frequently have lower levels of anxiety. In a similar vein, Emil Durkheim, in his epochal study of suicide, finds that higher levels of suicide are associated with "anomie," or the lack of consistent rules governing a society in change. He also finds higher levels of suicide in overly static, rule-bound societies where individuals perhaps more frequently cannot fully "be themselves." We can see therefore that social and cultural change can have strong effects on family dynamics--communication, mood, stability and cohesion.

Activity 45:
Try to assess the rate of cultural change surrounding and influencing a family you are aware of. Describe it.

How does this pace of cultural change affect this family?

How does the family attempt to cope?

Aesthetics

"Aesthetics" refers to the sense of the beautiful. Cultures define "the beautiful" in different ways. The sense of what is beautiful changes as culture changes with time.

The dynamics of aesthetics affect the family every day in multiple ways: clothing, hairstyles, body art, jewelry, décor, and tastes in music, movies and literature. Families can join together around similarities in taste, for example, the enjoyment of rap, wrestling or automobile designs. Or, this may be a source of conflict, as, for example, when "high art" proponents argue with "low art" proponents in the family.

Activity 46:
Give an example from a family you know. Give examples of...

a) **The family coming together around an art or aesthetic experience.**

b) **The family coming into conflict over art or an aesthetic experience.**

c) **What other functions does art and aesthetics serve in a family with which you are familiar?**

Time

The sense of time, its nature, speed and its precision, is very much affected by the socio-technical and thus the cultural environment. The sense of time in a culture will be very much reflected in the pace, precision, synchronization and pressure in the family.

Families may be operating in a slow-paced culture, perhaps affected by diurnal and seasonal rhythms; and families may operate in very high-speed environments where timetables are honed to minutes and multiple timetables must be synchronized. Families may operate in a "Third Wave" flex time environment, where meals, homework, work, leisure, sleep and love are "scattered" and moved around throughout the day giving a sense of "floating" or "unanchored" time.

Activity 47:
Think of a family you know. What is its relation to time?
How is it affected by its sense of time?

Interview an older person. Ask them if their sense of time was different when they were younger. Ask how this earlier sense of time affected family life.

126

Degree of Enculturation

In this we ask of the culture or subculture of which the family is a part, "To what extent are participants in this culture aware of other cultures? How much contact is there with other cultures? What is the attitude towards other cultures? Open or closed?"

Some cultures can be cut off and insulated from other ways of life, while others are aware of other peoples and their different solutions to the problems of living. Families with little awareness of other cultures, while they may have a sense of stability and identity, can be vulnerable and perhaps have fewer cultural resources to solve problems they might encounter.

On the other hand, families in cultures with many "cosmopolitan" features, who have a high degree of awareness of other cultures, may have a somewhat unstable "relativistic" view of their culture, but have perhaps a wider array of approaches to problems and challenges they may face.

Activity 48:
Think of a family you know. Does it have a wide or narrow array of contacts with people and experiences having to do with different cultures? What effects does this seem to have on this family?

"Race"

The word "race" is placed in quotation marks to indicate that it is a complex, constructed concept. This is, of course, true for many of the other concepts in this section--gender, age, sex and family--but the concept of race is so frequently and strenuously taken as an *a priori* category (something that really exists in the real) that the quotes are needed as a counterweight. Much could be written on this topic. Here, I will limit myself to a few points.

Societies vary in their levels of racism, the categories of "race" they use and the extent to which there is a widespread belief that "race" can be used as a predictor of behavior. Societies also change in their construction of race and the deployment of this concept. At one point in history, one's race may severely reduce one's social mobility, or one's choice of work or partner. At another, these obstructions may have lifted.

A family may be living as a set of first-, second-, third- or fourth-class citizens because of their physical characteristics. Families may be comprised of members of different "races."

Note that the concept of race is not the same as the concept of ethnicity. It is possible to be designated as coming from the same race and be seen as having different cultures. Black people are not necessarily "black," nor are white people all "white." Thus, two people may meet and marry and, while "racially" they are counted as different, culturally they may be quite similar. Cultures vary widely in the extent to which these slippages and complexities can be acknowledged. They also vary greatly in the attitudes toward such pairings--positive or negative.

Children seem to be born with no racial awareness whatsoever. These attitudes must be learned. Often they are learned with considerable force as the child enters the wider community, as they go to school as a young child, and encounter, in the classroom, on the playground, and in the street the racial attitudes present in their community. These form part of a nucleus of identity which is carried forward and combined with later experiences in adolescence and adulthood. These experiences are modulated, moderated and interpreted by the family.

Activity 49:
Think of a family. What are the attitudes it has toward "race"? How are these communicated? What function do these attitudes serve? What effects do these attitudes have?

Do you know a family with different "races" amongst its members? What effects, if any, does this seem to have?

Political Institutions

The manner in which decisions are made varies considerably from culture to culture. In some societies there is representative democracy and in certain communities individuals may feel that they can easily become directly involved in decisions affecting their lives—decisions affecting schools, land use, laws, pollution and so on. At the other extreme, there are societies in which such participation is unthinkable, where individuals believe, quite correctly, that these decisions will be made by others who wield power, and that they themselves have little or no influence over the outcomes.

The political process varies widely in many other dimensions; its formality, its history, the types of discussion and argument permitted, the language used and so on. These political dimensions affect culture and affect family life. The family will be affected in its management of authority, for example. Heads of households who feel they may affect their schools, communities and societies by political and legal activity will operate very differently from those who have given up or do not consider this possibility. These attitudes will affect the management of the family and will "rub off on" the children. Or a discontinuity may exist between the politics of the family and the politics of their community. This may result in estrangement, alienation, victimization or scapegoating. The political dimension of family life is usually overlooked but is worthy of serious consideration.

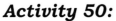

Activity 50:
Think of a family and its community. List the ways in which the family might get involved in politics (e.g. voting, joining a neighborhood committee, the Parent-Teacher Organization).

Write a comment on the nature of the list – is it long, short, varied?

Now describe the extent to which the family is involved in the political process and how much the family could be involved in politics. Write an assessment of how these factors might affect the family you are thinking about.

Individualism and Communitarianism

Running through many of the dimensions we have examined so far is the dimension that concerns individualism—the extent to which it is believed in the culture that people can "do their own thing" versus communitarianism – the extent to which it is believed in the culture that people should check out their actions with the community before they act.

The United States, for example, often manifests a highly individualistic culture. If an individual wishes to marry or divorce, quit their job, move across the country, start or end a business, they usually meet with an attitude of compliance from others, if not outright encouragement. In other cultures such behavior would be regarded as something wrong – it would be assumed that one should allow one's behavior to be controlled explicitly by others. Perhaps one's marriage would be arranged, one would be expected to stay in one's home town, follow in one's father's footsteps.

This cultural dimension has obvious and strong effects on a family, for the family system itself can become regulated by the community or, on the other hand, left to decide for itself how to operate. Recall too, that even in highly individualized middle class "western" societies, a form of communitarianism can occur when there is a strong culture of "keeping up with the Joneses," and maintaining a good social front.

Activity 51:
Think of a family. What kind of culture does this family inhabit? Is it individualistic or communitarian?

How do you come to this judgment?

Does your family "fit in" with its community, or does it seem to have a culture that is more or less individualistic or communitarian than its cultural surround?

What is the impact of the culture on the family in this regard?

132

Case Study: Nick

This case serves to demonstrate many of the processes we have been examining so far. It also serves to show how several cultural factors can play an active role in family dynamics. Read the case and answer the questions at the end.

Nick is a nineteen-year-old male who has shown up for counseling at a college counseling center. He complains of headaches, disturbed sleep and an inability to concentrate. His grades are slipping and he is feeling very confused. He was considering a medical career but is now not sure if that is what he wants to do. Perhaps it is more what his mother wants.

When he talks of his family he becomes quite tense. He is the first-born. He has a younger sister, aged 16. He reports that his mother seems frustrated and disappointed with his father, who has a job "hauling dirt." Nick seemed, during the first few session, to share this disparagement of his father, but lately in sessions, he seems more appreciative of some of his father's positive attributes--his thoughtfulness, persistence, toughness and durability.

When Nick first showed up at sessions he wore clothes that were too small for him, as if he had difficulty accepting that he had grown up. Recently he has been showing up in larger clothes, clothes that are more stylish. He states that he has picked these out for himself, while those he had before were selected by his mother.

Nick reports a dream. He is playing on a beach, quite involved in building sandcastles. He turns to call his father, only to find it is not his father but a rock. His father is nowhere to be found. He awakens, quite distraught.

He reports that he is attracted to girls, but that his mother believes he should wait until he is more established. Nick, however, is starting to wonder if he might go against his mother's wishes. Perhaps, he wonders, it would do little harm for him to date a little.

Nick reports having only a few friends currently. In fact, this pattern extends back into his childhood. His mother often felt, he says, that his friends were too low class, and that he was bound for better things. He notes, however, that several of these disparaged friends seem to be doing quite well.

Questions:

1. **What is the significance of Nick's clothing?**

2. **What life tasks does Nick face?**

3. **How is he doing in meeting these challenges?**

4. **What is the meaning of Nick's dream?**

5. *How is Nick's current situation shaped by his relationship to his parents?*

6. *How might cultural factors influence Nick's situation? Identify three factors from the list of cultural dimensions in this chapter.*

7. *What processes might be helpful in counseling Nick? Why?*

Attitudes toward the body

From place to place and through time cultures manifest varying attitudes towards the body. These attitudes are complex and multivariate, including attitudes regarding the body's ideal shape and size, how much of the body should be seen, what meaning is given to various parts of the body. Cultures vary in the extent to which people feel "embodied" or "disembodied"-- the extent to which people feel like they "belong in" or feel "at home in" their body. In some cultures, there is the expectation that one should override impulses from the body, and master the body. In other cultures such an attitude of hostility or control aimed at the body would be unthinkable. Cultures vary similarly in attitudes towards physical beauty and bodily markings, tattoos, scarification and so on.

The family will be affected by these bodily aspects of culture. Touching, body language, sexuality, demonstrations of affection will all arguably be affected by cultural assumptions about the body.

Activity: 52:
See if you can identify a cultural value in your culture that affects the body. Write it below.

Now write how this cultural feature might affect a family operating in that culture.

Love

Cultures have different attitudes and beliefs about love. Some cultures, for example, believe strongly in "romantic love," in its reality and in its importance in marriages. Other cultures might not regard "romantic love" as real or important. In such a culture people might not believe in "love at first sight," and consider marriages based on respect, friendship and teamwork more "real" than those based on "romantic love."

Attitudes regarding love change through time, are affected by historical events, economic conditions and cultural assumptions regarding individualism.

Activity 53:
What are the attitudes regarding love in a culture you are familiar with?

How might these attitudes affect a family living in this culture?

Work

Again, we have an exceedingly complex nest of cultural dimensions. In this complex we find factors affecting attitudes towards work itself, the so-called "work ethic." Much has been written on this topic by social scientists. In one set of attitudes we have societies that tend to regard work as something "transcendent" through which the individual realizes "higher" aims through work. This can sometimes be found in religious societies where God is served by work or in atheistic societies where the state, for example, might be served by work. In other societies work does not occupy such an exalted position--perhaps it is seen as a means to an end or even as something unpleasant, to be avoided. The roots of these attitudes perhaps lie deep in the complex history of a society. It does not take much thinking to see how the prevalence of such attitudes in the cultural surround of the family will affect family dynamics. Child-rearing will be affected. Core values influenced. The enthusiasm with which roles of provider are taken up and behaviors having to do with abstinence, discipline, planning, saving and impulse control will all be affected.

In addition to these fundamental attitudes towards work, culture is affected by the type of work the community is involved in. The culture of a South Wales mining town, where work is dangerous and physically exhausting is different from that of a dormitory suburb in the USA where people are involved in safe but often sedentary work. This is different again from rice farmers in Balinese villages where there is generally safe, physically demanding work, but work that requires a very high degree of respect for nature and extremely high levels of social cooperation.

The type of work will affect culture, and this in turn will affect the family. Sometimes these effects will be mediated by structural factors such as educational or religious expectations or requirements. Sometimes these work-driven elements of culture affect the family through the emphasis and induction of core values, courage, strength, intellectual agility, emotional containment and so on.

Activity 54:
Think of a family. What is the work its members are involved in?

      1.

      2.

      3.

      4.

What values are involved in this work and how do these values show up in family life?

Reality

Once again, we encounter dizzying complexity. Cultures vary in their conceptions of reality and in what constitutes reality. These assumptions have enormous impact on family life in a variety of domains: power and authority, sanity and madness, sound versus unsound decisions and so on.

In some cultures, reality is viewed as something that is socially constructed. In these cultures reality is often discriminated from the real. "Reality" is viewed as something made up of symbols, aimed at creating a picture of the real, but only a picture.

In other cultures this bifurcation of "the real" and "reality" is not acknowledged. The socially constructed reality, in these societies, is taken as the real. In these cultures, there may be a greater stability in knowledge or assumption structures, but the categories used and the assertions made are much more categorical, less negotiated, less open to change.

Families might be affected by such cultural dimensions, especially in regard to issues of non-conformity or ways in which differences between people are managed. A non-conforming individual in a culture adopting a more "constructed" view of reality may be dealt with more tentatively, with less cognitive certainty than in cultures where categories are more stable and taken as "real."

Activity 55:
Think of family. Assess the notion of reality that seems to dominate in this family. Is "reality" something tentative and open to question and uncertainty or is it settled, "taken as read"? Is it somewhere in between?

How do these assumptions about reality seem to affect family dynamics?

Separation - Individuation and Culture

Cultures vary in the extent to which they value "groupism" or individualism. Furthermore, other features of culture, society and economics profoundly affect the shaping of these cultural values.

These poles of groupism and individualism are paralleled by tensions within the family having to do with separation and individuation (individuals being their own person) and fusion or symbiosis.

These tensions can be poignantly seen in the toddler's striving for independence and in the adolescent's working towards autonomy. Both of these epochal conflicts are affected by factors operating in the broader society. Let us focus for a moment on adolescence.

An adolescent, for example, who resides in a culture that values both community and groupism, provides an array of opportunities for finding and being "oneself," provides for relative freedom of movement in travel, has an array of positive economic opportunities for which the adolescent has been prepared by an adequate educational system, does not impede separation via social defense mechanisms such as racism, ageism, sexism--would (in the absence of other predisposing factors, such as traumata in early life) be better able to traverse the late adolescent transition into young adulthood than an adolescent residing in a culture where the cultural, economic and social supports were not available.

The adolescent in the latter case finds himself trapped in the family, with no way out to viable young adulthood. Just as at the end of the Oedipal period, the child realizes there is no sexual future in the family so in late adolescence the individual, in certain cultures, realizes there is no economic, social or cultural future in the family. He or she must strike out. If this is not possible, the late adolescent feels as if s/he has no future, or, a future empty of supports. Conflict and disintegration, despair and apathy will often emerge in these contexts. Frequently they are seen as individual problems, sometimes as family problems. Occasionally they are seen as emanating from the broader social system.

Attempting to synthesize these thirty-one dimensions at one sweep is a dizzying prospect. It would certainly appear that cultural dimensions or schemas have potentially very powerful impacts on family life. Recall too, that each of these schemas itself is comprised of sub-dimensions, sub-schemas and all of these interact in very complex ways. Attempting to understand or manage a family without taking cultural variables into account seems very unlikely to succeed, if not doomed to failure.

Activity 56:
Intercultural Partnerships

Relationships between people of different cultures are increasing in frequency as global mobility increases. It used to be that intercultural partnerships were disparaged, but attitudes are changing as people realize that intimacy and caring are universal human needs.

In this activity you are to interview someone who is currently engaged in an intercultural relationship, (a) report on it and (b) answer a set of questions on it.

Directions
1. *Select an interviewee who is involved in an intercultural partnership. You may define for yourself the meaning of intercultural. It may be two people from different "races," religions, countries or even states.*

2. *Inform the respondent of the purpose of the interview and explain how you will ensure confidentiality of the results.*

3. *Conduct the interview in a secure, comfortable place. The interview should last 15-30 minutes.*

4. *If interesting questions emerge as you do the interview, by all means ask them if you consider them sensitive and appropriate.*

5. *As you do the interview, summarize back to the respondent what you heard them say, to ensure you are recording accurately.*

6. *Take notes in the appropriate spaces in the interview. Be sure to change names and other identifying information*

so as to preserve anonymity.

7. **Complete the reactions section of the activity.**

8. **Share your results and findings with others who have also done this activity.**

Interview
1. **How did you meet your partner?**

2. **In what ways are you and your partner culturally different?**

3. **How have cultural differences with your partner affected you?**

4. **What has been useful in dealing with your cultural differences?**

5. **What has not been useful in dealing with your cultural differences?**

6. **How have the attitudes of others affected your relationship, if at all?**

7. **As a couple, are you more influenced by your or your partner's culture?**

How?

8. **Has being involved in an intercultural relationship caused you to grow or learn new things?**

How?

9. **What challenges have you and your partner faced as a result of cultural differences?**

a)

b)

c)

How have you dealt with these?

Reactions
(To be completed later by the interviewer)

1. **In your opinion which of the following seems to apply?**

   a) **One partner has abandoned her/his culture in submission to the other.**

   b) **Both partners have given up their original culture and have taken up a third culture they both subscribe to.**

   c) **The couple is mutually searching for a culture that respects both their cultures fully.**

   d) **Each partner gives up something of her/his culture in a deal that involves important parts of their own culture.**

   What are specific examples that show this couple belongs to categories a, b, c or d above?

   What are the consequences of this?

2. **What have you learned from this activity?**

3. **What surprised you?**

4. **What questions are you left with?**

Case Study
An intercultural couple:
Mark and Natalie

Mark and Natalie live in Chicago, Illinois. They are 32 and 30, respectively. They have one child, Chloe, who is seven. They have been married for nine years. They met in college, where they were studying. Both work; he as a computer technician and she as a grade school teacher. Their marriage is stable and pleasurable for both of them, but some tensions and differences arise from time to time. Natalie's parents emigrated from Puerto Rico when they were in their twenties and Natalie speaks Spanish. Mark, on the other hand, is a third generation United States citizen and has a mélange of cultural backgrounds, mostly northwest European: Welsh, Scottish, German and Swiss. While, for the most part, they get on very well, they do tell of some conflicts they have had in the past and continue to have.

Natalie likes to spend a large part of the weekend with her family, celebrating birthdays, graduations, new jobs and so on. Mark's family lives over a large dispersed area, and Mark seems not to need so much contact with his family and would like less contact than they currently have.

They have different fighting styles. Natalie lets her feelings show and is quite passionate. Mark, on the other hand, can feel quite comfortable "sitting on his feelings" for days at a time and prefers to keep things cool. Natalie prefers not to fight in front of the children, while Mark has a policy of "transparency," meaning that he is quite happy to have children witness their fights, or at least most of them.

Natalie is very religious. She lights candles around the house and prays for her sick and dead relatives. Mark seems, at times, to ridicule Natalie's beliefs, and sometimes they have fights.

Identify how three of Mark and Natalie's issues might emanate from cultural differences. Refer to the list in the previous text. Identify at least three cultural differences.

a)

b)

c)

What might help mark and Natalie resolve some of their tensions?

CHAPTER 4
The Unconscious and the Family

Psychologists and other social scientists, as a group, are unsure of the concept of the unconscious. Some are not sure of its existence and many disagree on its nature. I am of the opinion that it is vital to take into account unconscious processes if one is to understand families, and that this is especially true if one is attempting to understand the more "unusual" phenomena occurring in family life.

Figure 1 gives a visual image of the unconscious in a hypothetical family. There are five members of the family, each represented by a small disc on the larger disc that represents the family "container" and its boundaries.

The small bubble over each individual represents the consciousness of the individuals comprising the family, and suspended underneath each small disc (in a hatched line, to represent its permeability) is a bubble to represent the individual's unconscious.

Hanging under the entire conscious system is a "group unconscious," the group mentality. This group mentality forms "under" any group that has reasonably well-defined boundaries and a set of shared tasks. A family is usually just such a group.

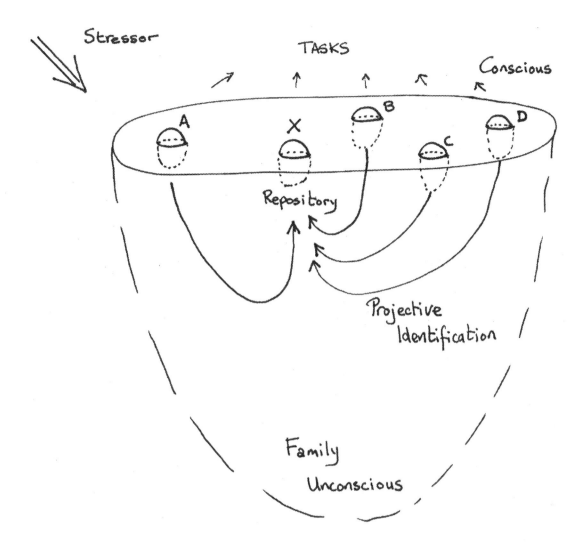

Figure 2: the Unconscious and the Family

Figure 2 also shows a very important feature of the unconscious of the group or family. It involves the process of *projective identification*. Projective identification occurs when individuals "send" unwanted parts of their unconscious, unwanted thoughts or feelings into others, as if to have them contain them. These receivers or *repositories* of unwanted parts are often used as scapegoats and are attacked. While they may be attacked, they are also usually preserved because they serve a function for others in the group and the group as a whole. Further, the scapegoat is unconsciously valued because he or she contains split off and projectively identified parts of the self.

An example may illustrate how this unconscious system works and how it may interact with the conscious system of the family.

Before we start, however, a few words about repositories. Individuals are more likely to become repositories (imaginary dumping grounds of unwanted unconscious feelings, thoughts and ideas) if:

a) they are the only one of a kind in a group; if, for example, they are the only woman, person of color or senior citizen;
b) they are low status, if they are "looked down upon" in the system;
c) they are at the boundary of the system, near the edge and have frequent significant interactions with things outside the system;
d) they have elements in their personality or their personal history that set them up to become a repository. These factors may include things like physical appearance, temperament, resemblance to other key persons in the family and personality predispositions.

Family as a Whole
CASE EXAMPLE: The Jones Family

The Joneses have been coming for counseling at your community mental health center for four weeks. The presenting problem is Jamie, 13, who has been failing at school, getting into fights and being very uncooperative at home. Her older sister, Hermione, 15, attends a school for the gifted and is very polite and studious. Geoffrey, at nine, is a lively, bright-eyed boy, getting "average" grades in school and displaying a respectful, sunny attitude.

Heather, 33, the mother, has a customer service job with a local community agency. It is demanding work and the hours are long. The hard work and strain show on her face, but she is extremely serious about doing well for her children. Heather describes her mother as "cold, selfish and mean." Heather feels she was always treated badly compared to her two sisters.

Heather's husband, Bob, has only shown up for two of the family sessions. He claimed to be busy, but the rest of the family reports that Bob rarely has a job and is unable to hold one for very long. He often gets into fights with bosses and co-workers.

When asked about this, the rest of the family seems not to display much feeling although you, as the counselor, seem to feel that there should be some intense feelings of anger aimed at the father. He seems to be more of a burden on the family and, with his anger, distance and his overly punitive attitude, gives little to the family while taking much.

When you ask the family who each member reminds them of, it seems significant that all the family agrees that Jamie is "just like Dad." They even claim she looks like him.

Much more will emerge over the coming weeks and months of counseling, but already, the counselor has enough information to develop a hypothesis regarding Jamie's behavior as explained by the concepts described in the first few pages of this chapter--group mentality, repository, projective identification and scapegoating.

The family initially adheres to explaining Jamie's behavior in terms of individual attributes, but a group-as-a-whole analysis yields some potentially useful insights and guides to action and intervention.

Activity 57:

In the space below analyze the Jones family utilizing group-as-a-whole concepts such as: repository, group mentality, scapegoating and projective identification. It is helpful to start with a group-as-a-whole stressor and trace the consequent feelings through the unconscious matrix of projective identification.

(On the next page, I have provided an analysis. Read this only after you have attempted your own analysis and compare it to your own.)

Analysis of Joneses
from a Family-as-a-Whole Perspective

First, we see that the whole family is under some pressure insofar as the mother has to work very hard to support everyone. There also appears to be a good deal of disavowed anger directed at the father. Furthermore, there seems to be a prohibition against speaking of this anger openly. Theoretically, this anger is then driven underground, into the group mentality. It is then projectively identified into a repository, who will then (imaginarily at first) contain the anger for the whole family. Persons of low status, who are isolated or one of a kind, persons who are located at the boundaries of a system, and persons who have pre-disposing personality or physical feature are frequently selected as repositories. The repository for the family stress and anger here is Jamie, the person who is seen as most resembling the father. She takes in (introjects) this re-directed anger, perhaps experiencing it as her own and becomes the angry child, getting into fights and being uncooperative. Although this might be explained as her imitating her father (so-called "modeling"), the dynamics being forwarded here are much deeper, more powerful and insidious.

With Jamie as a repository, the family now has a convenient target for its anger, a less frightening target than the father. The upshot is a stalemate, an unfortunate maintenance of the status quo, frustration, misdirected emotions and confusion.

In addition, it could be argued that Heather, the mother, is re-living, in her relationship to Bob, the negative experience she had with her mother--a form of repetition compulsion. Traumatized by much of what her mother did, but unable or unwilling to remember these experiences, she re-lives them by acting them out in similar form, with Bob, her husband. Again, theoretically, the more she is able to remember and "work through" the experiences at the hands of her mother, the less she will "accept" her relationship with Bob and the more she will push for a change. As she did this so the less would the need be to use Jamie as a scapegoat in the family. There is much work to be done examining the collusion, the unconscious "agreements" in this family.

This case, I hope, demonstrates how it is possible to explain family dynamics from a group-as-a-whole perspective, utilizing unconscious dynamics. Many phenomena that seem mysterious and intractable become clearer and open to change once this perspective is taken.

For a further elaboration on unconscious processes in groups and a listing of other references, you might find my book, *Imaginary Groups*, helpful.

This next case illustrates a dynamic discovered by Salvador Minuchin and described in his book "Psychosomatic Families," namely that family dynamics can influence bodily states and create a wide array of psychosomatic illnesses, such as asthma, and anorexia nervosa, where an individual refuses to eat and loses weight dramatically, sometimes to the point of endangering her/his life. It also illustrates that the precipitating stressor to a family need not always be that of trauma. A family could be stressed by ordinary developmental processes, such as an adolescent's pressing for increased independence.

Family as a Whole
CASE EXAMPLE: Andrea Wilson

Andrea Wilson is the oldest of three daughters of Bill and Tess. She has been diagnosed as anorexic. Although she is 16, and 5 feet 3 inches tall, she only weighs 74 pounds. Her sisters Beth, 14, and Mia, 12, are normal weight for their ages. Andrea is at considerable risk. It is decided that the whole family should see a psychologist, Dr. Viera.

In the sessions with Dr. Viera, it emerges that Bill is very busy and usually adopts a "hands-off," distant attitude towards his family. He is characterized as being "the strong silent type." Beth and Mia both seem quite happy and contented, except for their concern for Andrea.

Tess, the mother, describes herself as a "full-time mother," "devoted to her children." She says she is pained to see them grow up and is ferociously possessive of them.

The girls feel afraid of Tess, but also feel much loved by her. She monitors their behavior closely and chooses their clothes for them. The two younger daughters state that they do not feel constrained by their mother's attentiveness. Andrea feels differently, however, and sometimes puts up a fight, although usually to no avail.

Tess states she feels so close to her daughters, especially Andrea, and that she can "read their minds," that she "knows what is best for them" and can even sense when something is wrong with them when they are a long way away.

Andrea states that while she loves her mother, sometimes she would like to "be more of her own person." The mother becomes very cold and hurt at this unwanted expression of need for independence of her daughter.

Father does not usually intervene in these dynamics. Beth and Mia admit they sometimes let Andrea fight their fight for independence for them.

Tess reveals that she might hold on to the daughters so strongly because she lost her mother at an early age, when she was three.

Questions on Andrea

1.   *How might Andrea's anorexia be a manifestation of family-as-a-whole dynamics?*

2.   *How might the father, Bill, change his behavior to relieve some of the pressure on Andrea?*

3.   *What psychological issues might Tess have? How might they contribute to Andrea's anorexia?*

CHAPTER 5
Multigenerational Effects in Families

In some cultures, it is routine for people to remember the members of their family back for generations. Many people in industrialized cultures, however, will have to stop, in ignorance, after they reach their grandparents.

In many ways this lack of a sense of family history and an attendant detailed knowledge of the individuals involved, their struggles, trials, traumas and tribulations, is unfortunate; unfortunate not just in an aesthetic sense, or for a sense of roots (though these are important) but also insofar as many of these family experiences are transmitted across the generations.

There is considerable evidence that traumatic experiences are transmitted across generations in families. Much research, for example, has been done to demonstrate the impact of the Holocaust of World War II on children and grandchildren of those directly affected. Much research remains to be done on the exact mechanism whereby these experiences are transmitted. Much is done simply by conscious verbal communication. Much is probably also transmitted non-verbally. Perhaps some of the experiences are transmitted by unconscious communication.

These messages across the generations can often involve family secrets that unknowingly affect the family culture. The movie, "The Joy Luck Club," is full of examples of these experiences and messages being transmitted across the generations. Often against the conscious wishes of the mothers, the daughters would live out the "life scripts" of the grandmothers and great-grandmothers.

These transgenerational messages do not flow randomly, nor do they alight upon just anybody. The genogram is a technique that charts the generations of a family and, by asking a sequence of questions, helps clarify and explain patterns that exist in families across the generations.

Later in this chapter, we will examine the use and application of genograms.

So far in this book the bulk of our analysis has been aimed at two generations--parents and children--and clearly there are powerful effects operating here. In this section we will expand our focus and argue that some phenomena in families can only be adequately explained by taking note of multiple generations.

Many times, sometimes in an eerie way, a behavior, attitude or interest seems to be passed from generation to generation, sometimes against the conscious will of the individuals involved. A beautiful example of this can be found in the movie, "The Joy Luck Club," where we see trauma, expectations, and attitudes transmitted across several generations of Chinese and Chinese-American women.

Activity: 58:
Watch the movie, "The Joy Luck Club," and answer the
following questions:

1. *What examples do you see of patterns being repeated across the generations?*

2. *What happens when an individual attempts to change these patterns, to stop them from recurring in their life? Is it easy or difficult? Why?*

3. *What historical events seem to factor into these transgenerational patterns?*

4. *What cultural dimensions do you see operating in the movie? For example, do you see cultural factors having to do with gender, age, children, groupism, marriage and sex that affect these families over the generations?*

5. *What seem to be the messages conveyed by the movie? For example, is it possible to change these transgenerational patterns? What is the position of the family at the end of the movie? Is the family highly valued, or devalued?*

Case Example: The story of Bill
Unconscious transmission of trauma

I was born in 1947, two years after the end of World War II. Oddly enough, it was not until I was thirty-eight (after several years of psychotherapy) that I realized that, in a semi-conscious sort of way, I had felt as though I had been through World War II. It was as though I had, in some uncanny fashion, absorbed my father's experience. My father had been involved in D-Day, Arnhem, and the Battle of the Bulge. His health had been seriously damaged by the war and he had had to spend a year in a hospital after demobilization. Many of his experiences were traumatic, but he hated to even hear mention of the war. These shocks to his system remained inside, never to be fully "worked through."

Casting my mind back to my childhood, I recall that my father would never talk about his war experiences and would get visibly upset every time the topic came up, every time a war movie came on television. It was as if he contained unspeakable experiences. My theory is that my childhood mind absorbed these experiences, adopting them as my own as I identified, almost lock, stock and barrel, with my father.

Later, as my father began to speak more about his experiences, and I unraveled my relationship to him in psychotherapy, I came to take up the, at first, alien identity of a man who had gone his entire life without having participated in a war. I realized that without being aware of it, I felt as though I had been through a war, even though I had not. I even felt "military" even though I had never been in the armed forces. Upon further reflection, I realized that this had been going on for generations. My stepfather and his father, my grandfathers, and my step-grandfather all had been involved in wars, some spending almost their entire adult life at war.

Similar, but much more extreme, instances of this can be found in children of parents and grandparents who were involved in the Holocaust of World War II.

It appears that there is a form of unconscious identification of the child with the traumatized parts of their parents' personality and the child carries this introjected part of the parent as if it was their own experience. Alice Miller, in her book "Prisoners of Childhood: The Drama of the Gifted Child," alerts us to the fact that sensitive gifted children may be especially prone to do this.

Activity 59:
Think of an individual (either real or from fiction--a novel or a movie) whose parent has been through a traumatic experience. Does it seem as though the offspring has internalized this trauma? How? To what extent do they seem aware of it?

Imaging the Family

Sometimes we can get a different perspective on a family by creating an image. Following are brief descriptions of three methods for creating such images: the genogram, the kinetic family drawing, and the family sculpture.

Genograms

A genogram is a way of mapping multiple generations of a family, finding patterns and developing, as a result, explanations for behavior in the family. Drawing a genogram of a family nearly always reveals a new insight into family dynamics, especially with regard to intergenerational patterns.

The symbols: Below are some of the symbols used in drawing genograms.

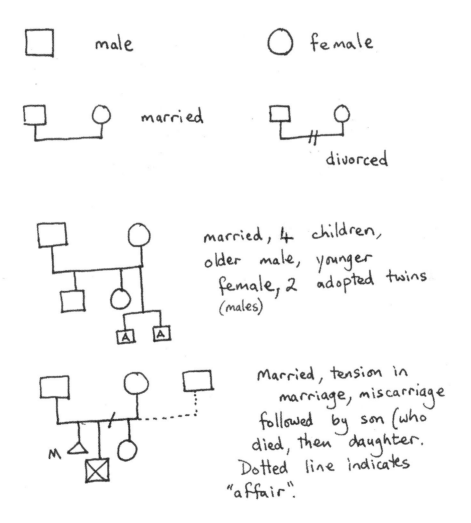

Figure 3: Genogram Symbols

In addition, you may list pertinent information, date of birth, education, occupation, health, etc. Be careful not to overcrowd the genogram with too much information.

Below is a genogram of three generations of a family. Ike, the youngest son of the Pearsons, has been getting into fights in school, has slipping grades and sometimes does not come home at night. In trying to explain Ike's behavior in terms of a genogram, we pay particular attention to:

a) conditions in the family at the time of his birth,
b) patterns involving birth order,
c) structural features that might "set up" the individual for certain projections and displacements.
d) conditions at the emergence of the problem

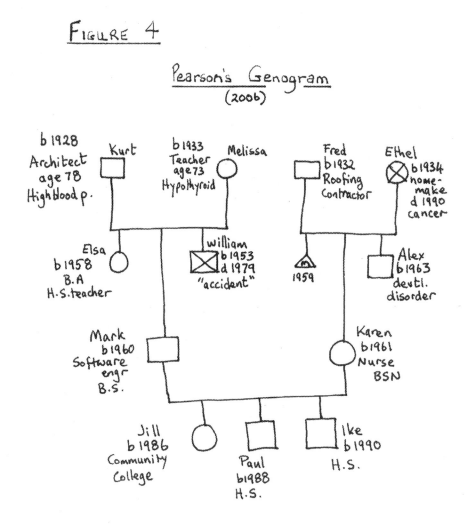

Figure 4: Pearson's Genogram (2006)

When we examine the three generations of Pearsons, as they are in 2006, focus on Ike and look for the patterns, the following features emerge that might set him up as the "identified patient."

First we note that Ike is the youngest son of Mark and Karen. There is a problematic pattern with regard to youngest sons in this family. William, Mark's younger brother, died at age 16 under mysterious circumstances, a fight at school that was deemed "an accident" by the authorities.

Karen's younger brother, Alex, has been diagnosed with "pervasive developmental disorder" since early childhood and Karen has had to do a lot of work involved in his care, especially since her mother's death in 1990. Alex lives in a long-term care nursing home. Ike is in exactly the same structural position as both William and Alex (that is, the youngest son). Unconsciously this could "set him up" for the role of "person with problems."

Ike is also 16. He is at the age that Mark's younger brother, for whom he felt responsible, died under violent circumstances. Perhaps there is an unconscious concern that history will repeat itself.

In examining the situation of the family at the time of Ike's birth, we notice he was born in the same year that Ethel, Karen's mother, died of cancer. Ethel was only 56 and Karen was very upset and depressed. She also had to "take over" care for Alex, who, up until then, had been living at home. These events would affect Ike and the family's relationship to him.

Thus, we can see, exposed in a genogram, how Ike might have been triangulated in a web of history, patterns and expectations that contribute to his current problems.

Activity 60:
Draw a genogram of your family or a family with which you are familiar.

Focus on one individual in the family, and ask these three questions:

a)   What were prevailing conditions in the family at the time of this person's birth?

b)   What patterns exist in the family regarding birth order? Who else in the family was in the same birth order, and how does the person-under-study's behavior reflect this?

c)   What structural features might set up the person you are studying as a target for certain fantasies or projective identifications?

d) What conditions existed as this person developed any problem they might have?

Answer the questions in the space below:

a)

b)

c)

d)

Now comment on the extent to which the genogram throws useful light on understanding the dynamics of the family.

Family as a Whole Genogram
CASE EXAMPLE : Terry Smith

The Smiths are considering going to counseling. More accurately, they are considering sending their nine-year-old son, Terry, to counseling. However, when they called the Community Counseling Center the intake worker advised them that they should all come in, the whole family. The intake worker suggested that perhaps Terry's issues were indicative of some issues existing in the whole family system. They did go to two sessions and the counselor was able to gather the following data.

The parents, Mark and Jocelyn, have been married for 14 years. They have 3 children: Harry, 13; Nina, 11; and Terry, 9. Harry and Nina appear to be functioning quite well. Their grades are B average and they have active social lives and pursue hobbies. Mark is a computer engineer, and works long hours as does Jocelyn, who is an accountant. They are financially comfortable and live in a five-bedroom house in a relatively affluent neighborhood. They are both white and describe their ethnicity as mixed European. Both sets of great-grandparents emigrated from Northern European countries-- Ireland, Germany, Poland, Wales, Sweden--and there is a family tradition of upward mobility and hard work.

Mark and Jocelyn seem to have a functional, businesslike relationship; they describe themselves as a "good team." However, both acknowledge that, about 9 years ago, around the time of Terry's birth, Mark was caught having an affair with a co-worker. He stopped the affair, but in the session, feelings still seem to be high. It was also at this time that Mark's mother was diagnosed with cancer. She died five years later.

Both couples describe troubled relationships with their siblings. Mark's younger brother is an alcoholic and relies on Mark to "bail him out of his frequent jams." Jocelyn's younger brother died 18 months ago. Jocelyn still is visibly moved when describing this event. She feels Ed, her younger brother, always got a raw deal in her family. She wishes she could make up for lost time.

Terry sat in the sessions rather vacantly. His "issues" started just over a year ago. He claims his parents started to pressure him at that point by placing him in honors classes. This disrupted his friendships and "ruined his life." His parents noted his resistance and hired a string of tutors--all to no avail. He started getting involved in conflicts at school and the parents deeply resented and feared this. They upped their control of him and punished him with groundings. The situation just got worse. The final straw occurred when Terry had a "meltdown" at home.

Questions on the case of Terry

1. *Events occurring around Terry's birth might have contributed to Terry becoming the identified patient, that is, the individual whom everyone sees as possessing the symptoms or problems in the family. What were these events, and how might they have contributed to this dynamic?*

2. *What factors related to birth order and gender might contribute to Terry's issues? How?*

3. *What "unworked," relatively unrecognized, difficult-to-discuss and emotionally charged issues seem to reside in the family unconscious?*

4. *How might Terry have become a <u>repository</u> for these issues?*

The Kinetic Family Drawing

This technique starts with the very simple instructions, "Draw your family doing something." The emphasis is on "doing" since the element of action in the drawing is revealing. It is important to emphasize that skill is not important, but that spontaneity is. The drawing can be of the family as it is now or as it was at a former time. Below, for example, is a Kinetic Family Drawing (KFD) drawn by a middle-aged man of this family as it was when he was nine years old.

Figure 5: Kinetic Family Drawing

Once we have the image, we can form hypotheses based on size, placement, activity and a host of other visual cues. In this image, we see the father and son engaged in a game of catch. The mother is preparing a meal and sister is playing on her own. The only two family members in relation are the father and son, and their relationship seems a mixture of cooperation and competition. The females are on the left of the picture, engaged in solitary activity and separate from the family. This family appears to be divided along gender lines. Also significant is the isolation of the sister. She is the only one facing away from the group. There is something forlorn about her. Also, we note a wall and a window separating the mother from the other three; somehow she seems cut off.

These observations can lead to hypotheses and those hypotheses can be tested for their applicability to the family. If they fit, they can be further explored. What were the consequences of this? What lead to this situation? How is my present situation defined by a past situation? What next?

Activity 61:
Draw a picture of your family (or a family you know) doing
something. Draw spontaneously and quickly, without
censorship.

Now, look at your drawing and make several observations.
Look for positioning, size, connections, areas that have be
crossed out, barriers and feeling tone. (Many more ideas
on how to interpret KFDs can be found in "Actions Styles
and Symbols in Kinetic Family Drawings (KFD), by Robert C.
Burns, Brunner Mazel, 1972).

Scan your observations and formulate several hypotheses
about the family process.

The Family Sculpture

For this technique you need several people. They can be either the family members themselves or others who represent that family member. In a sufficiently open space, ask the family people to arrange themselves, to position their bodies in such as way, as to represent their family. Once they have found their positions, they should hold them for a while, so one or more observers can walk around and look at the sculpture and formulate hypotheses. Further, this is a talking sculpture. People in it can be asked to talk about how they feel in their positions, how they got there, what the costs and benefits of their positions are and what they would like to do next, for example.

Such a concrete representation of the family can reveal very telling dynamics. People might feel like they are downtrodden, not seen or shut out and, while this might be hard to discern verbally, it can show up very dramatically in a family sculpture.

Be aware that this technique can be very stimulating and revealing. If you try it, be ready for some possibly dramatic and intense revelations.

CHAPTER 6
Psychological Type and the Family

The Myers Briggs Type Inventory (MBTI) is one of the most frequently used psychometric instruments in the world. It categorizes the person taking it into one of 16 personality types developed from four opposite pairs. No type is "better" than any other. Each type comes with its own strengths and vulnerabilities. These are widely written on. A good resource is *Gifts Differing* by Isabel Briggs-Myers. The theory is based on the study of personality types by Carl Gustav Jung. It is a "user-friendly" and non pejorative exploration of different personality types.

You can get a copy of the test, to find out your personality type, from a wide array of online sources, as well as from professional counselors.

While many aspects of family life are systemic, people do have individual styles and these can be interestingly captured on an instrument much like the MBTI. If we refer back to Chapter One of this workbook, we see that the elements of a system have properties. One of these properties could be construed as personality type. In exploring personality type, then, we are returning back to the attributes of the people comprising the family system we are examining. In so doing, we are not forsaking the systemic approach taken so far, we are elaborating upon it.

Many things that go on in families can be explained, at least in part, by using the concepts, categories and insights from the MBTI. Indeed, since the MBTI itself is based on the work, *Psychological Types* by C. G. Jung, a wide array of further interpretive avenues and lines of thought are opened up. For example, Jung's theory contains a rich interpretive scheme involving archetypes, the collective unconscious, and synchronicity and these concepts can be very helpful explanatory tools at times.

In this section, therefore, we will examine the four pairs of the basic dimensions of the typology, explore how these might help explain some dynamics of families, and further, examine how different psychological types might manifest themselves in family process.

Even if you have not taken the MBTI, you will still profit from reading on, since many of these categories and dimensions "make sense" and often people have a good intuition as to their type.

One determines one's type by seeing where one lies on four pairs of opposites, as shown below:

Extraversion...........Introversion
Sensing............Intuition
Thinking.........Feeling
Judging.............Perceiving

Extraversion - Introversion

This dimension has to do with the basic orientation of the personality. The extrovert directs their attention towards the outside world and the introvert directs their attention towards the inner world. Usually, but not always, the extrovert is outgoing and the introvert is more retiring. Jung felt that extroverts and introverts would often marry. Two married extroverts might compete for airspace while two introverts might drift apart. Furthermore, we often marry someone who is our opposite in terms of type so as to stimulate our growth, our self completion. Extroverts tend to reach out to other people for "energy" while introverts tend to look inside themselves when they need a boost.

Activity 62:

Are you more extroverted or introverted? Why do you say this?

Do you find yourself more attracted to introverts or extroverts? Why?

Does this agree with Jung's claim that we tend to seek out introverted partners if we are extroverted, and vice versa?

Is someone in your family an extrovert? How does this affect the family as a whole?

Sensing - Intuition

This dimension of Jung's typology has much to do with what types of information we regard as valid. Sensing types trust their senses. They rely heavily on sensory data and are thus very practical and often detail minded. Intuitive types, on the other hand, rely on imagination and are fascinated by possibility, by conjecture. They tend, therefore, to be more like "dreamers" or even visionaries. Two intuitives might forget to "read the small print" or to take care of everyday chores, and they may prefer new beginnings to mundane tasks. Two sensing types, however, may not "see the forest for the trees" and get lost in details. In this way, these two types need each other and profit from collaboration.

Activity 63:
Do you consider yourself more "sensing" or "intuitive," in the sense used by Jung? Why?

What are the consequences of this personal orientation...
    a.   *in relationships in your family?*

    b.   *in your career or as a student?*

Thinking - Feeling

This dimension, to simplify somewhat, has to do with the extent to which a person is ruled by logic (their "head") or by human values and feelings (their "heart"). The thinking type of person will face moral dilemmas, make decisions and comport themselves based on logic. The feeling person will see this as rather cold and unemotional, uncaring and diffident. Oftentimes, couples or parents and children will get involved in arguments over decisions that emanate from the different approaches of thinking and feeling. The thinking type may espouse a disciplinary system based on logic while the feeling type may find such an intellectual approach to human relations very unsatisfactory and alien.

Activity 64:
Do you think you are more of a thinking or a feeling type?

Give an example to illustrate how you are like this.

How do you like to argue...with logic (thinking) or with human values (feeling)?

Judging and Perceiving

The "judging" type of person prefers an ordered, predictable life; they plan and organize, they like to show up on time and keep to a schedule. The "perceiving" type, on the other hand, prefers spontaneity; they like to "hang out," to just let things happen; they might not mind showing up late or when plans go awry; they might even enjoy some chaos.

Again, these individual differences could show up in family life. One member could be "judging" (note: not judgmental) and like life to be orderly and tidy. Another member may be "perceiving" and like a more free-wheeling lifestyle. It takes little to imagine the conflicts that might emerge. "Can't you ever be on time?" exclaims one. "Can't you just relax and let things happen, go with the flow?" responds the other.

Activity 65:
Do you consider yourself more "judging" or "perceiving"? Why?

How does this affect the family you live in? Is this in conflict with members of your family?

Give an example to illustrate your assessment.

Psychological Type and Conflict

Following is a table of some typical conflicts between types. Some family conflicts can be usefully understood as conflicts based on type.

Extroverts will often say of introverts:
1   You're not expressive enough.
2   Why do I have to keep the conversation going?
3   Why don't you tell me how you feel?

Introverts will often say to extroverts:
1   Can we just be quiet for a while?
2   Stop pressuring me to open up.
3   Why do we have to communicate?

Sensing types will often say to intuitives:
1   Keep your feet on the ground!
2   Why can't you be more practical?
3   I need to <u>see</u> how it is done.

Intuitives will often say to sensing types:
1   Why do you have to be so practical?
2   Can't we dream and imagine?
3   There's more to things than meets the eye.

Feeling types will often say to thinking types:
1   You're so cool and aloof.
2   Not everything is logical, you know.
3   But what do you <u>feel</u>?

Thinking types will often say to feeling types:
1   You should think things through, and not be led by your heart.
2   I have feelings too, you know.
3   Your feelings aren't the best guide.

Judging types might say to perceiving types:
1   Could you get things done on time?
2   Will you make a plan, please?
3   We need to get this organized.

Perceiving types might say to judging types:
1   Can we just "hang out" and see what happens?
2   Can you be more spontaneous?
3   Let's forget the plan!

Alternatively, opposite types can be of great help to one another. Each can stimulate and support the growth of the other.

The extrovert needs the introvert to:

1 explore the inner world
2 interpret dreams
3 learn how to be alone and introspect.

The introvert needs the extrovert to:

1 connect with the outer world
2 join the group or the crowd
3 have fun with others, to communicate.

The intuitive needs the sensing type to:

1 be practical
2 read the contract
3 make the day-to-day things work.

The sensing type needs the intuitive to:

1 dream of the future
2 inspire
3 open up possibilities.

The thinking type needs the feeling type to:

1 help them understand others' hearts, to be warm-hearted
2 persuade others
3 make others feel wanted and important.

The feeling type needs the thinking type to:

1 analyze
2 finally make a decision
3 keep a cool head.

The judging type needs the perceiving type to:

1 have surprises
2 have new experiences
3 relax and be spontaneous.

The perceiving type needs the judging type to:

1 get organized
2 save time
3 realize goals.

These lists are just beginnings. I encourage you to read further. There is a bibliography at the end of this book on several topics, including the MBTI.

Case Example: The Bells and Psychological Type

Following is a description of the Bells: Richard, the father, Annie, the mother, Deirdre, the daughter and Ray, the son. At the end of the case, you will be asked several questions aimed at your ideas about their psychological types and how these affect their interactions. You will also be asked to come up with some ideas as to how they might be able to work together more effectively.

Annie: Strikingly beautiful, she has sometimes been called "the party girl." She is a very active and outgoing thirty eight year old. When the phone rings at home, nine times out of ten, it is for her. Often it is one of her friends, asking for advice on a relationship, or for a favor. Annie has a hard time saying no. She is often told by Richard that her heart is too soft and that people take advantage of her. Annie will bridle at this, since she is sensitive and very easily hurt, easily moved to tears. Annie feels pulled in many directions at the same time. There is never a dull moment in her life, although, at times, her family feels like they would like to spend more time with her, since she is so scattered. On the other hand, everybody's life in the family is enriched by Annie's "open door" policy wherein people often come to stay or "crash" in their house for a while. Open-hearted and generous, Annie rarely counts the cost, although she can be hurt deeply by people's ingratitude. She is often late, and this does not bother her. She is very confident interpersonally and makes friends very easily. She loves good food and drink, enjoys fine clothes and shoes. She loves sleep and can happily lounge in bed all day, enjoying relaxation as much as vigorous physical exertion. At these times, the housework will fall behind. Annie does not seem to worry about the mess.

Richard is a forty-five year old high school teacher. He has very few friends, although he is generally well liked. His moods are predominantly low key and cool. He rarely loses his temper or flies off the handle, preferring to deal with things rationally. He does have strong feelings, but they seem as though they are under the surface. It takes a while to get to know him. His family likes and loves him, but they will often jibe at him about the amount of time he spends reading, about his "absent mindedness," his "theory knowledge" and lack of "street smarts" or "common sense." Richard enjoys philosophy, science and history. Richard lives in a world of imagination, dreams and theory. He likes his life to have a routine, as if to stabilize some of his "loftiness." For this reason, perhaps, some of Annie's "scatteredness" has bothered him although he does acknowledge that he needs to "lighten up a bit."

Raymond, eighteen, likes to keep to himself and to "keep things basic." He spends many hours cleaning, repairing and tending to his car. He has a steady girlfriend whom he loves intensely and protectively. He enjoys her because she is quiet and unintrusive. She seems to understand him without his having to talk about what is going on inside of him. He has a small circle of friends who really like him but often will state that they find it hard to know what is really going on in his head. "Still waters run deep," they say. Academically he runs into problems since he does not see the purpose of most of the curriculum. For him, learning should be practical. It should solve a problem you have in your life right now, or why bother? Theory is just so much fluff from his point of view. His parents, who have high hopes for him, get very concerned with this attitude and there have been several fights over his "not trying hard enough" at school. He enjoys physical comforts, and this seems to be the way to let him know that you care for him. Words don't seem to do much, but actions, such as a ride to the garage, or a favorite meal, count for a lot. His fights with Richard are particularly distressing for the family. Richard confronts Raymond and attempts to pursue the argument to a rational conclusion, but Raymond gets very upset, confused and explodes in an emotion, often storming out of the room, overwhelmed with feelings—feelings that he will not put into words. These fights are followed by long stretches of silence as the two hurt and angry men circle one another, keeping their distance.

Deidre, 12, is bright and vivacious, always on the go. She hates to be alone and inactive. When she is with her friends, she comes alive. She will play fantasy games with them for hours on end, making up stories and acting them out. She often will compete with her mother for use of the phone, in hopes that the call is for her. At school she does very well in the activities that involve language and vocabulary. She is several grades ahead in this regard. She shows a remarkable ability to grasp quite adult concepts in the conversations she will often have with her father when they walk home from school together. Both seem to derive considerable satisfaction from this. She also shows an almost uncanny aptitude for identifying with the feelings of others—a pronounced capacity for empathy. Richard recalls how once she exclaimed that one of the children was talking about how their grandmother had recently died and that she, Deirdre, found herself crying as if it was her grandmother! There are numerous examples of such events as these. At times Deirdre thinks she is odd, but Richard and Annie take pains to explain to her that it is a special, albeit a painful, gift. There are fights over messiness, however. Deirdre keeps her room in a permanent state of mess and, since she likes to go off and play with her friends at the drop of a hat, the mess will accumulate until it reaches imponderable proportions. At these times there is usually an intense fight. When she fights with her mother, it is a straightforward explosion of feeling. When she fights with her father, she explodes in tears and emotion, while he attempts to reason with her, usually to no avail.

Questions on the Bells:

1.   **What psychological type is each of the Bells? Write a short justification for your choice.**

Annie
Type_____

Richard
Type_____

Raymond
Type_____

Deirdre
Type_____

2. *Describe two tensions in the Bell family that emanate from differences in psychological type.*

A.

B.

4. *Give the Bells two pieces of advice, or two insights having to do with psychological type, that might help their functioning. State why you think it will help.*

A.

B.

CHAPTER 7
Love

Types of Love and the Family

It takes a certain audacity to take up the topic of love, yet no discussion of family dynamics is complete without some attention paid to this, for love is, in many instances, what holds the family together.

The focus here will be on the love adults have for one another. The approach is informed by psychodynamic theory and the ideas of Sternberg (1988).

Sternberg forwards the idea that love can be seen as being comprised of three components:

1. Intimacy involves the sharing of oneself, one's feelings, thoughts, attitudes and possessions with another. Another aspect might be emotional closeness or contact.
2. Passion involves physical, sensual, sexual or erotic attraction to the other person.
3. Commitment involves the decision to stay with the other person. This can range from no commitment to short-, medium- or long-term commitments.

Sternberg places these three components in a triangular relationship as on Figure 6.

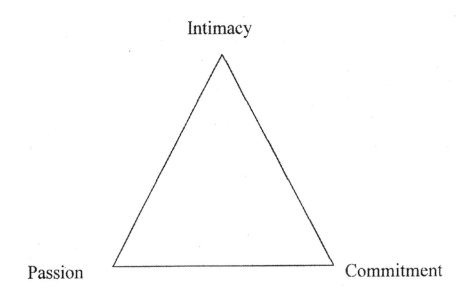

Figure 6: Sternberg's "Triangle of Love"

In addition, Sternberg argues that, by "mixing" these three basic ingredients, seven types of love (if one includes "liking") emerge. Further, an individual, or a couple can locate themselves in or near one of these seven types of love. These are diagrammed in Figure 7.

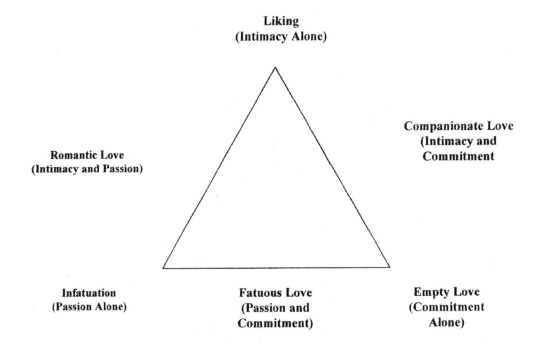

Figure 7: Kinds of loving

Let us briefly describe the seven types of love on the diagram above. **Liking** is, strictly speaking, not love, since it involves no passion or commitment. It is more like the friendship one might feel for an acquaintance, or someone one has to work with, someone, who is "OK." **Companionate love** can be found in couples who are close and have decided to stay together, but who feel little or no passion for each other. They are more like "good friends." **Empty love** would be found in a relationship where there is little or no emotional closeness and all that is holding the relationship together is the will of the partners to stay together. **Fatuous love** is a "shallow" love where the pair feels passionately about each other, has decided they will stay together for a long while, but does very little in the way of sharing. They know next to nothing about each other, beyond the fact that they are attracted and committed. **Infatuation** is here defined as when the love involves passion alone; no commitment, no intimacy, just passionate attraction. **Romantic love** here means the lovers are passionately attracted to one another, share intimacies, but have not made any long standing commitment to the relationship.

Not shown on the diagram above is the ultimate mixture of the three vertices, namely, **consummate love,** where one has, so to speak, "hit the jackpot," one is passionately attracted, able to share intimacies, and committed to the relationship.

Factors affecting love choice

Where one locates oneself on the triangular "map" of love found in Figure 7 is affected by many factors. It is a dynamic process, ever evolving throughout the life course and the stages of the family. Following is a list of some of these factors.

> **A: Culture** can affect one's location on this triangle. Some research shows that in lower income, collectivistic cultures the emphasis on romantic love is lower, while in higher income, highly individualized cultures (like the U.S.A.) romantic love is more important.

> **B: Early attachment** can affect the nature of one's later love relationships. Researchers have found that there are several modalities in which infants and toddlers feel attached to their caregivers (anxious, secure and avoidant, for example) and that these early patterns of relatedness "map forward" into adulthood. The toddler who is <u>secure</u> in their relationship to their mother is more likely to feel secure in adult love relationships. The child who is <u>anxious</u> about their relationship to their mother will be likely to replicate this in their adult love relationship (by showing anxiety over departures, absences and abandonments, for example), and the child with <u>avoidant</u> attachment (a child

who has been so much abandoned that they seem to have given up on human connections) will tend to live a remote, disconnected lifestyle with little love and often great isolation, but not experiencing (at least consciously) the anxiety, loneliness and fear of the anxiously attached child.

C: Fixations and Developmental Impasses can impact where the individual locates themselves on the triangular map of love. For example, an individual who has not resolved Oedipal issues (as described later in this chapter) may find it hard to commit to an intimate relationship out of guilt or fear of unconsciously hurting their same sex parent or because of frightening phantasies of their angry retaliation.

D: Trauma can affect one's positioning on the triangular map of love. Illness, losses, accidents, bombings, economic depressions and so on affect our fortunes and our emotional expectations and can cause us to adopt self-protective stances towards others (perhaps out of fear of getting re-traumatized) and these show up in how we love, or keep our distance from, others.

E: Life stage development affects one in very complex ways. People, for example, may "decide" not to "be in love" for a certain period of time because they have important other life tasks to accomplish, such as building a career for themselves.

An individual who has not achieved a sense of separation and individuation may suffer anxieties over getting close to another person out of a fear of being engulfed. They may then, self-protectively, keep their distance.

An impasse or derailment in any of the childhood and adolescent life tasks posited by Erikson (trust, autonomy, initiative, industry and identity) can all interfere with establishment of love and intimacy.

There is a plethora of developmental theories. All of them contain elements to explain the form of adult love relationships. H.S. Sullivan and his explication of the "chum" stage of pre-adolescence shows us how early love in friendship can lay a bedrock for later sexual intimate relationships. Children who are isolated, ostracized and lonely in, say, grade school may have difficulty falling in love later on.

The list of potential derailments on the way to love is so long. No wonder it is so prized when it is finally found. For others, they may undergo a "sea change" at, say, midlife and become much more "romantic" or more "pragmatic" in their expectations of a love relationship. People also resolve earlier difficulties and developmental derailments, just as broader social conditions can change to edge an individual towards or away from different forms of love.

Activity 67:
Thinking of either yourself or of someone you know (real or imaginary), locate them on the triangular "map of love." Answer the following, as they fit.

Why do you place this person there?

Is the person they are with in the same region?

Do you see connections, like the ones just described between culture, developmental impasses, traumata, attachment and life stage development and the preferred style of loving in adulthood?

CASE EXAMPLE: Nick and Irene

Nick and Irene come to counseling complaining that their relationship has come to a standstill. They have been living together for four years, but somehow seem unable to make the "next step"—to buy a house together, to get married and have children.

Nick is a photographer who seems on the verge of becoming famous for his artistic portraits. However, he, at age 39, feels his life has amounted to nothing and states that he is "very impatient to move on with his life." Irene is a graduate student in social work, committed to helping the homeless mentally ill on the streets of her city. She often feels unsupported by her teachers and supervisors.

Irene is puzzled as to what is causing the standstill in the relationship. She seems very self sufficient and seems not to place too many demands on Nick. Nick is "tired of waiting" and is frustrated by Irene's slow progress through school, and with his own felt lack of career progress.

Nick and Irene first met in high school and were attracted to each other, in part, because they both felt like outsiders. They became comforting companions, each helping break through the other's sense of isolation.

Nick describes a situation which is typical of his relationship to his father. Nick invited him to a public showing of his photographs. It was very prestigious, but his father was very lukewarm in his response. Nick feels his father has always been more excited by his sister's productions.

Irene describes her parents as "near catatonic—completely lacking in animation—like the living dead," and claims they have been that way for as long as she can recall. She and her two sisters learned to never rely on their parents for any kind of support or emotional contact. The sisters turned to each other for help, took care of themselves, or simply went without. Irene's mother has bee hospitalized for schizophrenia several times. In sessions, Nick and Irene seem to generously respect one another and it seems they certainly feel very warmly toward each other. Their love perhaps has been buried under other prevailing issues.

They are both verbally fluent and intelligent. Nick once tested with an IQ of 150. Irene is somewhat more "flat" and measured in her demeanor. They both would like to "move ahead," but are stuck, frustrated and confused.

Questions:

1.   *What type of love do you see in the relationship of Nick and Irene? Do you think their conscious feelings might be different from their unconscious feelings? Why?*

2.   *What issues from their families of origin (i.e. the families they grew up in) seem to be carried forward into their current relationship?*

3.   *What "psychological types" (using the typology of the preceding chapter) are Nick and Irene? How does this affect their relationship?*

4.   *If you were their counselor, what approach would you take? Why do you think this would work?*

Common Tensions in Heterosexual Relationships

Nancy Chodorow's theory, which seems to so powerfully explain and describe so many of the common tensions that are found between men and women, is founded on the following conditions in society.

a) Society has a heterosexist agenda. There is a goal, transmitted to children, that they should grow up to become heterosexual and that gender roles should be differentiated along fairly stereotyped lines.
b) Most of childcare, especially early childcare, is done by women.
c) Children are typically <u>gendered</u>, that is, introduced to notions of gender difference and how the genders are to behave, at approximately three years of age.
d) Prior to three years of age, children form a <u>primary maternal identification</u>. They identify with, become one with, in some ways think they are, the person who is taking most care of them, usually the mother.

These four conditions are sufficient to set in motion and to explain dynamics of heterosexual relatedness that are familiar, perhaps all too familiar. The story of boys and girls runs as follows:

Little boys, from birth to the age of three, typically are identified with their mothers. Not yet having gone through the process of <u>gendering</u> they have primary maternal identification. This is displayed by the child feeling at one with the mother, symbiotically fusing with the typically female mother, melting into her, becoming her, becoming female. This changes at three when, typically, the boy is encouraged to behave like a boy and to separate from his mother. The boy is encouraged to repress this identification with his mother, to cut his ties to her and to connect with the masculine world. He is encouraged to repress and suppress all the trappings of this maternal identification, and may even encounter shaming if he remains or "slips back" into being a "mother's boy."

Later on, this will manifest itself in an anxiety in the man of anything that is reminiscent of primary maternal identification. Such things as emotional closeness, intimacy, softness, caring and nurturance will, while being deeply desired by the young child in the man, be rejected by the gendered boy and man. This internal conflict leads to stereotyped ambivalence and anxiety found in men as they relate to women, living out the script of "go away a little closer," often to the puzzlement of women whose story is quite different.

When the little girl, at age three, is gendered, and "discovers" she is a girl, she is not caused to forsake her early identification with her mother and is not disparaged for being "mother's girl" as would be a boy for being a "mother's boy." Given this, the girl can base her identity on the firm ground of an identification with the mother.

Later on, as a woman, assuming a reasonably good relationship with the mother, there will be little anxiety over intimacy, a more secure sense of gender identity, less ambivalence and ambitendency in sexual relations, and an increased capacity for thinking critically about sexual relationships.

Further, in later life, the "opposite" gender carries a different symbolic meaning for men and women. For the girl, the male stands for, in part, the father. The father "shows up" as an object of affection and dependency usually at about age three, which, developmentally speaking, is quite late. This emergence of the father at about three years old has to do with common culturally-driven roles for men in child rearing. Namely, the father is relatively distant during the early and serving the function of "separator from the mother" somewhat later. Thus, the woman is relating to the male from a position of relative maturity and self-differentiation. This is even more the case if the woman, as a girl, had a satisfactory relationship with her mother and is not seeking to compensate for an early lack in her maternal relationship by having the male, boyfriend or husband, stand in for the role of mother.

On the other hand, the man, in relating to a woman, is in the position of relating to a person who symbolizes the mother and thus the very earliest stages of life, rife with issues of dependency and potentially life-threatening helplessness. The male, thus, while being attracted to the woman, is also fearful of the potentially powerful regressive tug that the woman represents. This dynamic is represented in much popular culture and ancient mythology--Odysseus and the Sirens, to name but one of many examples.

These dynamics again help explain many of the classic tensions that exist between males and females, especially in heated heterosexual and authority relationships.

In addition, I would like to point out the gender differences created by these dynamics insofar as they affect different capacities for males and females to undergo a therapeutic regression.

Several theorists argue that, as we grow up, we are "provided with" several opportunities to regress and re-work old repressed issues and attempt to resolve them, thus giving ourselves a fresh start. It is as if life has a certain generosity, by providing the individual with the opportunity for "do overs" for second chances at life.

Examples of points of regression would be the two years or so prior to puberty, of which Peter Blos writes so evocatively; late adolescence and the famous midlife crisis.

Now, if the previous formulations are true, then the girl, when provided with these opportunities for reconstructive regressions, will be more able (other things being equal) to regress to earlier ages since to do so will not jeopardize her gender identity. She will not, by virtue of psychologically venturing close to or even into the realm of primary maternal identification, fear that she will lose her gender identity. Thus, if a girl has issues focused on the first three years of lie, she is (*ceteris paribus*) more able to explore them.

The boy and man, on the other hand, when confronted with these opportunities for self-reconstruction through regression may be more careful, especially when considering regression to very early eras of life--eras suffused with primary maternal identification. To regress to these eras is to risk his gender identity in a society that frequently punishes men who become "feminine."

These processes would result in men often being more psychologically "vulnerable" than women, insofar as they contain "capsules" of early trauma--complexes that have not been worked through, despite being offered opportunities by normative regressions in life. These "capsules," however, can emerge on the scene if the (biopsychosocial) stress is sufficient. Often these will occur in the form of a "breakdown," substance abuse, violence against self or others or psychosomatic illnesses, to name but a few.

Women, on the other hand, will generally have fewer such unworked capsules, unless they have had very painful early childhoods, in which case they would psychologically resemble men in this regard. In addition, women, under stress, are often more likely to make contact with others which buffers their stress.

These dynamics help to explain the litany of statistics on gender differences regarding violent crime, domestic abuse, sexual predation and so on.

Chodorow's theories and the extensions I have added to them help explain and codify many of the stereotyped tensions we find in heterosexual relationships. I provide a beginning list below.

Stereotyped (Socially Constructed) Tensions in Heterosexual Relationships

   a) She has feelings, he avoids them.
   b) She longs for intimacy, he fears it.
   c) He thinks clearly, she floods with emotion.
   d) He is independent, she is dependent.
   e) He is strong, she is weak.
   f) He acts, she feels.
   g) He longs for autonomy and achievement, she fears it.

Activity 67:
Think of a heterosexual relationship with which you are familiar.

Can you find three ways in which it "fits" the preceding ideas? Write them below, if you can.

     A.

     B.

     C.

Now, thinking of this same relationship, are there ways in which this relationship <u>does not</u> fit with the previous ideas? Why do you think this is so?

Love and Repetition

What follows is an attempt to understand romantic love and patterns of love. This daring attempt will combine a number of different frameworks of analysis: attachment theory, psychodynamic theory and existential theories. I will start this complex synthesis with a case--it is a composite of one I have frequently encountered in my practice. It is so frequent that I have dubbed it with the ironic label "Bad Boyfriend Syndrome" or "Bad Girlfriend Syndrome." I will sketch out the feminine form in what follows to help in exposition.

Bad Boyfriend Syndrome

A young woman, Stephanie, 28 years old, shows up in counseling. She looks very depressed and tears up easily when she starts to talk about her life.

Her major source of pain currently is in her relationship with her boyfriend, Steve, whom she loves even though he does not treat her well. He exerts a strange but powerful attraction on her. She describes a typical date. She goes with Steve to a bar where they have a few drinks. Steve bumps into an old girlfriend. Before she knows what has happened both Steve and the other girlfriend have disappeared. Steve's friends at the bar kid Stephanie about where "Steve is now." Broken-hearted, crestfallen, angry and forlorn, Stephanie goes home to her apartment to try to cry herself to sleep. Shortly after 2 a.m., Stephanie's doorbell rings. It is Steve, drunk, apologetic and seductive. Against part of herself, her better judgment, she lets Steve in. They have sex. He spends the night. When he leaves he says he will call soon. Days pass and no call. She slides further and further into an angry depression. Finally, she decides to go to counseling, and here she is.

Further inquiry reveals that this is a common pattern for her in love relationships and that she is getting anxious about ever finding anyone reliable, falling in love and settling down.

She describes another man, Tom, whom she knows through her work. Tom is very interested in her and has asked her out on a date several times. She finds Tom "boring." In describing "boring" Tom to the counselor, however, it turns out that he is a complex and deep person, with a broad array of active interests. He does not seem "boring" at all to the counselor. He certainly seems worthy of a date or two, at least for exploratory purposes, but Stephanie resists him.

This is a puzzle, or it was a puzzle the first few times I encountered it in my practice. Hoping not to sound too arrogant, I think I have a solution to this riddle. Why does Stephanie (or "Bob," or the "Stephanies and Bobs of the World") continue to seek out a painful relationship when a perfectly satisfactory alternative is available? Why does Stephanie fall in love with the "wrong person"? Why can't she leave him? This string of questions opens up two quotes. First, from Camus:

> "All our life is a quest for the person in the presence of whom our heart first opened."

and second, from Santayana, the philosopher,

> "Those who cannot remember the past are condemned to repeat it."

Picking up the thread offered by each of these quotes, we can find our way to a useful formulation to help explain "looking for love in all the wrong places."

The First Opening of the Heart

First, let us attempt to unravel the quote from Camus. When do we first open our hearts, and to whom do we open it?

We often can remember our first loves, but we love before we can remember. We loved on the other side of the amnestic barrier that for so many people is erected at about 3 years of age. It is hard, for most people to remember before the age of three, and yet, so much of importance, that will affect our love lives, happens then.

We cannot interview babies, but much research and observation points towards the first opening of the heart occurring very early in the first year of our lives, as we attach emotionally to our caregiver (usually our mother). Camus could be arguing, as would a depth psychologist, that although we leave this first love relationship we are committed all our lives to re-discovering it or a likeness of it in that special someone who makes us feel that same profound and primordial sense of connectedness.

If it was a sense of connectedness... For sometimes this early relationship will get derailed and it will be both the connectedness and the derailment that will be sought and relived.

But why would we seek to re-live a derailed relationship? This does not make sense. It would make sense to avoid these painful experiences. Santayana's quote offers an explanation, but just the fact that Santayana says we repeat that which we cannot remember and that we cannot remember very early childhood does not make it so.

An idea of Freud's steps in here to help explain--not only to help explain but also to offer a way out (not an easy way out but at least a way) of interminable repetition of the same old pain, the same old frustrations. This idea is the idea of **repetition compulsion.**

The idea of Freud's is found in his seminal article, "Remembering, Repeating and Working Through." In it he argues that humans, when subjected, in a condition of helplessness to a traumatic experience, will frequently repress this memory to the unconscious so as to forget it. They then will seek to repeat the experience in various ways so as to gain a sense of mastery over the experience. As the individual becomes more able to <u>remember</u> the experience (often with the assistance of analysis or therapy) so they are less compelled to <u>repeat</u> it. It is as if memory substitutes for repetition.

Now we have enough intellectual equipment to return to the puzzle of Stephanie and her behavior. The formulation is as follows: Stephanie is returning to Steve and Steve-like men as a way of repeating unremembered traumas from her childhood. This formulation also provides a way out. If she can <u>remember</u> the precipitating trauma (and talk about it), she will not have to repeat it and she will be free to seek more satisfying relationships.

This remembering will be painful. The freedom memory provides is gained at a cost--the cost of sadness, re-experienced fear, remorse, depression. Further, even as remembering weakens the drive to repeat so anxiety is stimulated by the thought of connecting with a more satisfying person, for example, Tom. For to connect with Tom is to connect with a good person, a person whom one might lose. One opens oneself to being re-traumatized.

There is a temptation to return to the comfortably uncomfortable, but familiar relation with Steve or his likeness.

Interestingly, the original trauma for Stephanie and others is not always with her father. Stephanie describes her father as a kind, easy-going man, always ready to listen or lend a helping hand. Her mother, however, is an alcoholic and has been since Stephanie's early childhood.

Thus, Stephanie's first love was an alcoholic--perhaps available at times and at others remote and heart-breakingly unavailable. In loving Steve she is re-experiencing her relationship with her mother; perhaps even in the hope that she will be able to reform both Steve and her mother and even re-write the history of her childhood.

Further, when she goes with Tom she feels on some level that she is leaving her mother, not her real mother (who probably would approve of this high status relationship) but her internal mother. Stephanie must cope with abandonment anxiety each time the relationship with Tom starts to go well. This abandonment anxiety she masks with a defensive sense of boredom and at times she is tempted to give Steve a call. Perhaps, with time she will be able to separate from this internal alcoholic mother and start to live more freely, more on her own terms.

This rendition, focusing on Stephanie and "bad boyfriend syndrome," could be reversed. We could examine Steve in a similar fashion, tracing his relationship to Stephanie and other women back to his early childhood loves and pains.

Relationships are reciprocal and multi-layered. Satisfying relationships often provide the right mixture of repetition, so one feels a secure sense of the familiar and of hope for the new, hope that repetitions that are tired and run down will be replaced by the new.

One hypothesis emerging from this line of thinking is that it is extremely important that we treat children with warmth and consistent empathy if we wish them to find satisfying love relationships in adulthood.

Activity 68:
Think of an adult you know. Attempt to describe the pattern of their love life. Ask, "Is this pattern in any significant way repetition of aspects of their early childhood?"

Activity 69:

Love, Marriage and Culture

Individuals have different attitudes towards love and marriage. These differences are often affected by cultural factors. This activity will help get you in contact with some of your assumptions in these domains. (At the time of going to press, only heterosexual couples could legally marry in most countries. For the purposes of this exercise, assume the term "marry" includes homosexual pairings.)

1. *How important is <u>being in love</u> in your decision as to whom you should marry? (Circle one.)*

Not important at all		Somewhat important		Very important
1	2	3	4	5

2. *If a couple is no longer in love, how strongly do you feel this justifies their getting a divorce?*

Not strongly at all		Somewhat strongly		Very strongly
1	2	3	4	5

3. *To what extent is it OK for a couple to not be in love, but to be "good friends"?*

Very OK		Somewhat OK		Not OK at all
1	2	3	4	5

4. *Reflect on your responses and write several sentences, giving the reasons for your answers.*

5. *Now discuss and share your responses with several (3-5) others who have also answered these questions.*
   a. *What did you learn?*

   b. *What surprised you?*

   c. *Were there differences among others that seemed to be affected by:*
      i) *Culture?*
      ii) *Gender?*
      iii) *Age?*

6. *How might people's responses to these questions (questions 1-3) be affected by:*
   d. **Relative income levels?**

   e. **A culture of individualism?**

   f. **A culture of groupism?**

7. **What questions are you left with?**

CASE EXAMPLE: Ted and Marylin

Marylin is confused. She has been married for 15 years to a man in a comfortable relationship. Now, at the age of 40, she is considering divorce. Ted, her husband, is a decent man and they are "good friends" with a lot in common. However, they feel little passion for one another. They rarely have sex, even though both are attractive and healthy.

She feels at odds with herself. Why does she want to leave? Ted is not abusive or alcoholic or mean. It's just that he is somehow not exciting or emotionally available. She feels lonely and tempted to have an affair.

Ted is confused by Marylin's dissatisfaction. He does not want to change the relationship. He enjoys its friendly basis and feels no need to make it more passionate or erotic.

Marylin grew up in a comfortable suburban neighborhood. There were no childhood losses of great moment, or illnesses, substance abuse or physical violence.

What Marylin does report, however, is a chronic, cool remoteness from her mother, a distance that made her feel continually lonely in her childhood, lacking in warmth, empathy and emotional contact. She felt like she had been placed in the "wrong" family through an error at the maternity ward. She is surprised by her current attraction to a sensitive, empathic and sensual man.

Questions

1. *Using concepts from this chapter, explain Marylin's relationship to Ted. Where was it located on the triangle of love?*

2. **What early childhood experiences may have led to this love-choice?**

3. **What seems to be happening to Marylin currently, and what tensions is this creating in her marriage?**

CASE EXAMPLE: Ben

Ben is a strikingly handsome 45-year-old man. He complains of a deep, despairing loneliness. He has never been married, has had many girlfriends, but the relationships only lasted a few months. He is puzzled as to how he ended up at this point in his life. He is intelligent, accomplished in his career and well-spoken. He would love to have a family, but something always seems to go wrong with his love life. Often, it seems as though he unconsciously sabotages these relationships, as if he doesn't deserve them or as if there was an unruly part of him that somehow emerged and spoiled the relationship.

When remembering his childhood, what stands out for him is his mother's controlling of him, her lack of understanding, and her deep contempt for his father, who worked with his hands, in a brick factory. It was dirty work, his father did, and Ben himself came to feel ashamed of him. He was to be the fulfillment of his mother's dreams. He felt, in this way, as though he had replaced his father.

He never had girlfriends during adolescence. He reports having "crushes" on several girls, but he felt paralyzed with shame over his father's job and anxiety over his fantasy that his mother would get enraged should he bring a girl home.

Questions

1. *How might Ben's childhood and adolescent experiences in his family be affecting his adult love choices?*

2. *What developmental steps might he need to take to improve his love life?*

Oedipal Resolutions and Love Choices

The Oedipus complex of Sigmund Freud has occupied much attention of psychologists and other social scientists. It has been described in a multitude of different ways by a wide variety of thinkers. In this section, I offer another rendition of the Oedipus crisis in childhood, offer some ideas on how it might impact an individual's love life and offer two illustrative case studies. This account is a simplified one; much is being left out.

The Oedipus Stage

Between the ages of 3 and 6, a child develops an erotic tie with (usually) the parent of the opposite sex. They simultaneously start to feel competitive impulses, perhaps destructive, towards the parent of the same sex. The child also starts to feel that the same sex parent will perhaps retaliate and harm them, thus preventing them from staking their claim to the prized and beloved parent.

Eventually, the child encounters the incest taboo and is forced to relinquish his original aim. A sense of defeat and despair ensures, to be replaced by the realization that, if one identifies with (becomes like) one's erstwhile enemy (namely the same sex parent), one may eventually lay claim to one's original desire, the opposite sex parent.

This identification is a crucial forward step in psychosocial development. The child is opting to mature, to take the long way to his or her object of desire, accepting "civilization" and forming ambitions and aims. Societies typically capitalize upon this ambition and malleability in the five- to six-year-old child and start schooling, either formal or informal.

Much occurs on either side of this crucial developmental epoch but the contour, texture and tone of this period can have tremendous impacts on later love life.

Optimally, the Oedipal stage can operate like a "workshop" where all participants learn about basic human propensities, such as love, hate, rivalry, winning, losing, restraint, magnanimity in victory, mastery of ambivalence, playing by the rules, forgiveness, jealousy and compassion, to name but a few. Thus, under optimal circumstances a child can emerge from this stage strengthened and wiser in their capacity to cope with these powerful and potentially disruptive emotions, and is thus better prepared to cope with society and love relations in general. Further, the successful resolution of the Oedipal complex implies that the child accepts that there is no erotic future in the family. If he or she is seeking sexual gratification in a love relationship, they will have to look outside of the family.

Under sub-optimal conditions, however, this developmental bounty is not to be found. Following are some examples of how the Oedipal stage might get derailed. A father, for example, might be very vulnerable, and competitive. Instead of enjoying the competition from the prince, his son, he is threatened and retaliates vengefully, perhaps criticizing the boy, reducing his self-esteem or hitting him and frightening him. Thus, the boy may suffer a poor self-confidence in love or fear attacks should he make his love, his desires, explicit.

A mother may be similarly competitive with her daughter and create a similarly low level of robust self-confidence. Perhaps a mother disparages her husband and worships the son, who then feels as though he has "won" the Oedipal battle. It is, however, a Pyrrhic victory, for he has not "really" won, nor is the way out of the Oedipal stage, namely identification with an admired father, available to him. This boy may have difficulties leaving home from a clinging mother. When he considers bringing home a girlfriend later on, he may become very anxious insofar as his having a girlfriend implies that he has rejected his mother. He may become afraid of her wrath.

A father, instead of simply enjoying his daughter's "I love you, Daddy!" may take advantage of the situation. Perhaps he uses this love to further his narcissism, thus impeding the girl from transferring her love to other men. Perhaps he is so needy and fearful that he predates upon the girl sexually and thus causes a collapse in the symbolic/imaginary Oedipal drama and development is seriously derailed.

Variations on a theme

Frequently, people ask about single-parent families. "How can there be an Oedipal triangle if there is only one parent?" This is an important question because single parenthood is often the case. I usually respond that no studies I have encountered convincingly show that spending one's Oedipal period in a household with one parent demonstrably derails the Oedipal resolution. This is because frequently other figures are around who excite these issues and even if there are not actual people available, there are images of people that serve, to some extent, the same function. A mother, for example, may share treasured memories of her father or brother and implicitly communicate that this is someone who has her heart and with whom the son may compete and, ultimately, identify.

In addition, life provides many "do overs," many opportunities to regress and recapitulate, to finish unfinished business. During the period prior to puberty, for example, there is a normative regression when children will re-activate earlier fixations. Unfinished Oedipal issues may manifest in the form of "crushes," "puppy love," and bouts of jealousy and rivalry.

Another common question has to do with sexual orientation. Freud felt that homosexuality was, to a large extent, created in the Oedipal crisis. This belief is currently challenged by thinkers who argue that sexual orientation is determined at birth (or genetically, constitutionally) and that the child enters the Oedipus crisis with sexual orientation already set in place. This has the effect of changing the Oedipal story to one where, for example, the boy is attracted to his father and competitive with his mother, with whom he eventually identifies. One outcome of this (as presented by Richard Isay in *Being Homosexual*) is that the boy may be rejected by a homophobic father living in a heterosexist society. This potentially adds a trauma and further difficulties to the tasks of the Oedipal stage. Lesbian girls entering the Oedipal period would arguably feel attracted to their mothers and competitive with their fathers. The complexities of the situations following on from this would be worthy of a book parallel in form to Isay's.

As we have already seen, identification is a multi-layered phenomenon. The Oedipal identification overlays and interacts with the "primary maternal identification" of very early childhood.

Sometimes the passage to the phase of identification at the end of the Oedipal period is thwarted, resulting in an <u>Oedipal fixation</u>. Oedipal fixations can take on a number of forms. They may manifest themselves in an individual who always has to be in "love triangles" or in a person who continually has to make "conquests" in the field of love; or it may show in extreme sexual competitiveness, seductiveness, flirtiness or in an anxiety regarding sexuality, love and romance. The exact nature of the fixation will depend on the circumstances in the Oedipal situation the child finds themselves in, along with a host of other variables, not least among them, the culture the child grows up in. For example, a mother may disparage the boy's father and treat the son as her "little man." This may give the boy a fleeting sense of Oedipal victory, but in the end he loses because there is no way out for him, for to identify with his father is to become like a disparaged man and is to abandon the mother, who may react angrily.

A father may react to the daughter's love anxiously. The mother may become very jealous and competitive, and the daughter comes to feel that there is something wrong with her love, and fearful that others may harm her if she should act upon it. The Oedipal drama, comprised, as it is, of a triangle offers infinite dramatic possibilities, possibilities that never cease to entertain, amaze or strike us with awe, whether they occur in reality or in romantic comedies, or in the great tragedies.

Following is a case to illustrate some of the ways in which Oedipal issues might influence later love relationships.

CASE EXAMPLE: Lois

Lois is an 18-year-old Puerto Rican college student. She complains of a deep depression following a breakup with her boyfriend, a 32-year-old graduate student.

She describes her mother as a mousey woman, unable to stand up for herself, especially in regard to her father whom she describes as very full of himself, very self-involved.

She is interested in drama, music and performance art and is working on a group project at school. She is becoming attached to the teacher, a man in his forties, apparently well known in the college for his flamboyance and radical views.

She is unsure of how to be. She reports going to a party, planning on wearing a revealing dress and being the center of attention. Somehow she was not able to "pull it off" and she is left feeling very "out of it--invisible." At times like these, she thinks of just quitting school and going to take up some nondescript job.

In recent sessions she is starting to get in touch with some deep anger at her father. At these times she also has more sympathy for her mother. She describes her father at these times as very self-centered, lording it over her mother who, it seemed, did nothing to stand up for herself. She suspected her father of having numerous affairs and this hurt and angered her deeply.

Upon reflecting more recently, however, she recognizes her mother had been, and still was, a caring person, who volunteered for several community organizations.

Lois vacillates between feeling quite confident about her future--her future in love and work--and feeling very despondent and hopeless.

Questions

1. What life tasks does Lois face? (See Chapter 2)

2. What challenges is she facing in meeting these tasks?

3.   *Do you see signs of an <u>Oedipal fixation</u>? How? What may have led to this fixation, if you see one?*

4.   *How does Lois' relationship to her mother explain some of her present-day behavior?*

5.   *How does Lois' perception of her parents' relationship affect her today?*

6.   *What might a counselor do with Lois that might help her resolve these issues?*

7.   *Review the case of Nick (earlier in this book). Do you discern any Oedipal issues in his case? How?*

Engulfment and Abandonment in Love Relationships

Intimacy is complex. People seem to long for it and yet fear it at the same time. This ambivalence leads to many kinds of tensions in love relationships. Murray Bowen, a noted proponent of the intergenerational understanding of families, has argued that the couple, as a couple, faces the twin anxieties of engulfment and abandonment.

On the one hand, we fear getting too close because, although we might love to "lose ourselves" in another's embrace, at the same time we fear such a loss as dissolution. Would we be safe "inside" the other person? Would they let us go? Would we be able to retain our separate identity, or would we lose our individuality? These anxieties arguably build upon the resolution of our first separation from our mothers, so aptly described by Margaret Mahler (1978).

On the other hand, when we become intimate, we take a risk; we invest a person with importance, we rely upon them. While this reliance is essential, it also evokes anxieties of abandonment, fears that we will be left alone.

In response to these anxieties, people make a range of adjustments. Some swear off human intimacy, keep their distance, and protect themselves. Others might get involved but only if they have a "back-up plan" (often another person). Instead of forming a couple, they form a triangle. The third point in the triangle helps protect from feelings of engulfment or abandonment. Perhaps many "triangles of love" are formed on this basis. Sometimes, however, the third apex of the triangle can be a parent, or a job, a child, or an addiction.

Activity 70:
Think of a love triangle you have seen (either in reality or in fiction). To what extent does the idea that a love triangle can serve as a protection against anxieties to with engulfment or abandonment seem to fit?

Activity 71:
"Scenes from a Marriage"

This fine movie, directed by Ingmar Bergman, depicts the dynamics of a Swedish married couple. It opens as they are interviewed by a television crew, ostensibly as an example of an ideal couple--modern, egalitarian, self-actualizing.

This is followed by several delicate scenes where problems are touched upon but swept under the carpet. Ultimately, these problems and issues emerge in a dramatic way and we witness painful emotional wrestling and self-exploration. This movie provides a sensitive and delicate close-up of a couple's dynamics.

The following questions may help highlight some of its especially interesting aspects:

1. *What are early signs that there are unrecognized tensions in their relationship?*

2. *In what ways is their relationship affected by their culture? (Refer to the list of cultural dimensions in Chapter 3).*

3. **What type of love relationship do they have according the triangular model of Stenberg? (See the beginning of this chapter).**

4. **In what ways did the couple's childhood relationships to their parents affect their marriage?**

Projective Identification in Love Relationships

In the chapter on the unconscious and the family we encountered the concept of projective identification. We saw that, among other things, it is a way for people to rid themselves of troublesome feelings, fantasies and impulses by having someone else act as a container for them. This process not only occurs within and between groups. It is also a very powerful unconscious process operating between couples. For example, one partner might feel very uncomfortable with their strong impulses. They may then projectively identify these impulses into their partner, as if to say, "I can't handle these; you hold on to them for me." Perhaps the partner obliges, obliges even to the point of acting out these impulses both for themselves and for the partner. When this happens, when they get drunk or angry or wild, the projecting partner may seem outraged but behind the scenes may feel gratified as they live, through the other, that which they will not permit themselves.

Perhaps the partner who is at the receiving end of this projection has some unwanted parts of their own to trade. Perhaps their life history has left them feeling very uncomfortable with their intellect. perhaps it was threatening in their family of origin. Now, it is as if they project their intellect into their partner, as if to say, "I am ill at ease with my analytic skills. You hold them for me." The partner is perhaps all to ready to take up and contain these unwanted pieces. Perhaps because they serve well their intellectualization which acts as a defense against their impulses and urges.

Thus the deal is locked in. The couple may continue in this fashion for years in a state of equilibrium, until something happens that operates as a deal-breaker. Mid-life might bring an awareness that time is limited and a wish for change. Perhaps a depression sets in, organized around the missing functions, or maybe another relationship stimulates an awareness that perhaps one can lay claim to and safely live out the previously projected parts.

It is often at just such points of disequilibrium that couples need counseling and that counseling can help in the reclamation of disowned parts of the self and the re-establishment of the relationship on a new footing. Much of the time these couples make these rearrangements on their own, although it is not as easy as it might sound at first blush.

CHAPTER 8
Gay and Lesbian Families

In very few parts of the world (as this goes to press) are marriages between same-sex partners regarded as legal. However, gay and lesbian couples do form partnerships, and have children and thus form families.

Very little research or work has been done in this arena. This chapter is not intended to be a compendium on this emerging topic. It is intended to open up topics and ideas to stimulate curiosity and further exploration of this domain.

This chapter will examine two topics: a) the idea of the extra developmental task imposed by a heterosexist society on the gay or lesbian individual, and b) an examination of a case study of a lesbian couple and their two children.

The Extra Task

Armand Cerbone (1995) presents the idea that the gay individual or lesbian in a heterosexist society, has, in addition to the developmental tasks described by Erik Erikson, further tasks, often centering around "coming out" to a society that is frequently unaccepting, if not downright hostile.

As we examine each of the Eriksonian stages in turn, we can see how extra tasks are added or extra stresses exerted at each stage.

i) Trust - Mistrust
    In coming out, the gay or lesbian individuals places themselves in a vulnerable position, a position that calls upon deep resources of trust in themselves and others.

ii) Autonomy vs. Shame and Doubt

Coming out in a heterosexist society will expose these individuals to a greater than usual amount of shame and doubt, placing more strain on their drives towards self-regulation and assertion.

iii) Initiative vs. Guilt

Heterosexist societies will routinely induce guilt in gay and lesbian individuals for their sexual preferences, and, following Erikson, this will place stresses and strains on the development of initiative.

iv) Industry vs. Inferiority

Again, the negative pole of the Eriksonian "dialectic" is potentially emphasized as the gay or lesbian person comes out and s/he is led to feel inferior.

v) Identity vs. Identity Confusion

The task of forming an identity is rendered more complex and emotionally charged for the gay or lesbian individual. In a heterosexually biased society, integrating one's gay or lesbian sexual orientation into one's identity does not usually meet with social approval or a wide array of socially sanctioned role models around which one may organize a provisional identity.

vi) Intimacy vs. Isolation

Given the lack of legal and other social and economic supports for gay and lesbian partners, and given the social disapproval for public displays of affection between gay and lesbian couples, establishing an intimate relationship can be more difficult than it already is for the gay and lesbian individual. For these reasons, an additional vector of difficulty is added to this, as to all the other Eriksonian tasks.

vii) Generativity vs. Stagnation

Access to certain positions and roles is frequently not granted to gay and lesbian individuals (and of course to many others who are marginalized or excluded). Often, these roles provide avenues for generativity, for care for future generations--roles like minister, executive officer, senator, professor, mentor, youth group leader, coach. For Erikson, these are not just high-ranking economic opportunities; they are avenues for the discharge of the genetically determined drive to care for the young, and the future of society. Deprived of these opportunities, the individual can "dry up," wither and die a sort of "spiritual death." It is this risk the marginalized individual faces to a higher than usual degree.

viii) Ego Integrity vs. Despair

In this stage, the individual puts her/his life together, to see the big picture. For an individual whose attempts to accomplish the previous seven life tasks have been thwarted owing to societal pressures and prejudices, there is an extra task; extra effort must be made in order to achieve the necessary dignity of integration.

Cerbone's ideas perhaps provide a useful tool for sensitizing us not only to gay and lesbian issues but also to those of any group or person excluded from vehicles that enable the surmounting of Erikson's developmental program. As discussed earlier, these developmental dynamics will show up in the dynamics of the family.

Activity 72:
Think of a movie, play, novel or news item that involves gay or lesbian individuals. Briefly summarize it below.

1. Does this item illustrate Cerbone's ideas on gay and lesbian development? How?

2. In what ways does this item demonstrate ideas beyond Cerbone's?

CASE EXAMPLE: Nina and Trish

Following is a case example of Nina and Trish, a longstanding lesbian couple who come to see a counselor with several presenting issues. This case is not intended to be representative of lesbian couples or parents. It is presented as what it is, a unique family, containing, within its uniqueness, elements found in many families. The questions at the end explore these ideas.

Nina and Trish identify themselves as a lesbian couple. They are 37 and 35 years old respectively and have lived together for 16 years. Trish is very athletic and works out a lot. She likes to compete in triathlons and ultra-long cycle races. She makes many attempts to enter the world of work but, as yet, nothing long-lasting has materialized for her. This places her in something of a dependent relationship to Nina who is a hospital-based physical therapist, and makes a good salary. They have two adopted children, Nancy, 8, and Elise, who is 5.

When asked by the counselor, they report that their problems are mainly between themselves. The children seem to be doing fine. They get good grades in school, eat, sleep and play well and show nothing that a clinician might call "symptoms." Nina and Trish, however, seem very "stressed out." They fight a lot, mostly over money and responsibilities. Nina complains that Trish is a spendthrift, buying unnecessary luxury items on a whim, and that she seems unable to settle down and get a "real job." Trish, in response, gets guilty and teary-eyed and then resentful, and then they as a couple seem to get locked into a battle where Nina plays the "Parent" and Trish is the rebellious adolescent "princess." At these points the fights escalate and they look to the counselor for help.

Trish comes from a wealthy background. Her father was a successful industrialist and was always ready to step in to help her when she ran low on cash. She is an only child. Six months ago her father died. She claims that she has adequately mourned his loss.

Nina comes from a family that sounds very violent and abusive. There is a strong impression that she, as a child, had to cope with much emotional turbulence and potential violence--perhaps by becoming a "super child" and growing up very quickly.

They are both extremely busy. There is a lot of work to be done by both the adults, involving their careers and the care of the children. They have a good number of fights over the responsibilities for the work.

The tension seems to be confounded by their spending habits which typify the old saying, "Champagne tastes, beer budget." They live in a very expensive neighborhood and buy only the best, and this places a lot of pressure on them to generate cash. Much of this pressure falls on Nina, who is the major breadwinner.

Their communication style is quite functional, most of the time. They do listen attentively, but as soon as emotional tension rises they revert to "taking a stand" and defending themselves, and the discussion grinds to a halt.

At times, when a problem is resolved or when there is a moment of mutual understanding, one can discern a deep tenderness amounting to love between them, and this, combined with their energy and sense of humor, comprises a great deal of their strength as a couple.

Questions

1. *How might issues emanating from Nina and Trish's "family of origin" be contributing to their current problems?*

2. *Comment on Nina and Trish's achievement of the major life tasks of career and intimacy. What blocks do you see, and what may have contributed to these blocks?*

3. *Do you see any of the dynamics in this case as being specific to a lesbian couple? How and why? Could a similar set of problems also be found in a heterosexual couple or a male-gay couple?*

4. *Do any of Cerbone's ideas seem to apply? How?*

5. *If you were the counselor to this couple, what approach might you take?*

CHAPTER 9
Theory of Positive Disintegration and the Family

Many of the phenomena we encounter in families can be usefully explained when we apply the concepts, ideas and hypotheses of Kazimierz Dabrowski's theory of emotional development, the theory of positive disintegration.

I have used this theory, in my other books, to explain other phenomena, for example, group processes and the experience of emptiness. In this chapter, I will give a brief description of the theory of positive disintegration (the same one used in my other books, *The Experience of Emptiness* and *Imaginary Groups*). Then we will examine several of the ideas in the theory as they can be applied to explain fairly common occurrences in family life.

Theory of Emotional Development or The Theory of Positive Disintegration

The theory of positive disintegration, or aspects of it, is delineated in a number of volumes including Dabrowski, Kawczak and Piechowski (1970) and Dabrowski and Piechowski (1977).

The theory of positive disintegration (TPD) states that there are five hierarchically organized levels of development. The process of development involves a transcending of an earlier structure through its disintegration and ultimate restructuring into a new structure. Thus, disintegration is seen as positive, as being a necessary process for development to occur. One of Dabrowski's books is entitled *Psychoneurosis is Not a Disease*. In it, he argues that many things that are understood as "neurotic" are, in fact, breakdown phenomena resulting from emotional development; they are signs that psychological growth is occurring.

The Levels of Development

Level I - Primary Integration:

At this level the person is organized around the meeting of basic survival needs. The person at this stage feels relatively well integrated, and has as his primary purpose the meeting of "instinctual needs," e.g. hunger, sex, safety, shelter, comfort. It seems as though the person is dealing primarily with what Maslow (1968) termed "basic needs" and not "meta-needs," or higher level needs. The individual at this level of development is unaware of meta-needs, or if he is aware of them, assimilates them to his primary orientation of meeting basic needs. This would occur in much the same fashion that Kohlberg (1976) has demonstrated that people of lower levels of moral development interpret and assimilate the acts of higher moral development entirely in the terms of lower moral development. That is, for example, they may interpret altruistic acts as being acts of meeting basic needs. Level I is the level of the confident, unconflicted, self-serving individual. They are untroubled by a conscience or concern for others.

Level II - Unilevel Disintegration:

At this level the relatively smooth functioning of Level I breaks up, disintegrates and leaves the person with a predominantly wavering attitude. The previously well-bound and integrated structure now becomes loose, resulting in the individual feeling attacks of directionlessness and chaos. There is a difficulty in making decisions; forces within the person push against one another so that the person vacillates. In the absence of an internal hierarchical organization (the disintegration is unilevel) the forces do not resolve into smooth and deliberate action. The person at this state is very subject to polarities of emotion. Sometimes the disintegration can be extreme and result in psychosis. In other instances, the person can "pull themselves together" and manage to function in a seemingly integrated way. Under pressure, however, the disintegration returns. Frequently people at this stage long for a return to the "good old days" of Primary Integration, when things seemed, by comparison, simple. The words of Yeats' poem (1989) seem to capture Unilevel Disintegration quite aptly:

> "Things fall apart, the center cannot hold,
> Mere anarchy is loosed upon the world."

The hallmarks of this level are ambivalence, mixed feelings, ambitendency, confused and conflictual activity, and the sense of having multiple selves. The individual is unsure as to what is really important, as to what should take precedence.

222

Level III - Spontaneous Multilevel Disintegration:

At this level of development, things are still fallen apart, but there is a growing hierarchization within the person. Instead of equipotent forces acting upon each other, resulting in a wavering, vacillating directionlessness, there is a developing sense of a hierarchy of values, with certain values and forces emerging as prepotent. The person begins to feel "inferiority towards himself," that is, he starts to experience the difference between what he is and what he ought to be. This develops out of the newly-emerging hierarch of aims and values. Among some of the other "dynamisms" (or experiences that can facilitate and encourage further development) are: positive maladjustment, feelings of guilt, feelings of shame, astonishment with oneself, hierarchization, subject-object in oneself, inner psychic transformation and self-awareness, self-control, autopsychotherapy and education-of-oneself.

Level IV - Organized Multilevel Disintegration:

In this stage the person has developed an organized and consistent hierarchy within him or herself. In the words of Ogburn (1976):

*"He has transcended the problem of becoming
and tackles the problems of being."* (Ogburn, 1976)

The basic needs are generally well taken care of at this stage or have receded into the background; the individual is concerned largely with the meta-needs that Maslow speaks of. (Maslow, 1968, p. 210) In fact, Piechowski (1982) argues that there is a strong correspondence between the Self Actualizing person of Maslow's thinking and the person who has achieved Level IV. Thus, some of the active dynamisms are: self-awareness, knowledge of one's uniqueness, developmental needs, existential responsibility, self-control, regulating one's own development, education-of-oneself, self-induced programs of systematic development. The primary task of the individual at this stage of development is to solidify the structure that emerges from the previous disintegrated stage.

The locus of control (that is, whether they feel they are directed from within themselves or without) for the individual at Level IV is very firmly an internal one-he can act independently of the external environment if he so chooses.

Level V – Secondary Integration:

Only a few rare individuals reach this level of development. At this stage, the "ought" has become unified with "what is." The personality ideal has been achieved. The planful self-development of Level IV has been successfully completed. Individuals at this level seem to experience self, other, time, being and the world in radically different ways. Thus, persons at the other levels often have difficulty understanding them.

Overexcitabilities

Development through the stages is related, in large part, to the level and profile of excitabilities in the person. Dabrowski posits five types of overexcitabilities: Emotional, Psychomotor, Sensual, Intellectual and Imaginational. An overexcitability is a predisposition in the individual, largely inherited, to respond to certain types of stimuli in an above average manner. For example, a person with sensual overexcitability will be more responsive than average to cutaneous stimulation. He or she will also tend, if this tends to be his or her dominant type of overexcitability, to transform other types of experience, (e.g., emotional, intellectual, imaginational) into sensual types of experience. For example, the emotion of affection will be readily transformed into stroking for a person with sensual overexcitability.

Perhaps another term for overexcitability would be sensitivity, perhaps analogous to photographic paper which can be varied in its sensitivity to various types of light input. The pronounced overexcitability would correspond to a finely grained, highly sensitized paper-the impression of reality gained when there is an overexcitability that is correspondingly sharp, intense and vivid.

Following is a brief overview of the manifestations of the various forms of overexcitabilities (OEs):

Sensual: This manifests through a heightened sensitivity to sensual experience—skin stimulation, sexual excitability, the desire for stroking, physical comfort, tastes, sights, colors, etc.

Psychomotor: This manifests itself in a tendency for vigorous movement, violent games and sports, rapid talk and a pressure to be moving. Emotional excitement is converted into movement that is highly charged with energy. Dancers and athletes might have a high degree of this OE.

Imaginational: This is shown in a sensitivity to the imagined possibilities of things. There is a rich association of images and metaphors flow freely. People with high levels of this OE might easily confuse reality and imagination.

Intellectual: In this the individual displays a voracious curiosity and desire to learn and understand. There is a persistence in asking probing questions and a reverence for logic. There is a love of theory and an enjoyment of thinking.

Emotional: This is the most important overexcitability in that if this is absent or weak, it is unlikely that development will proceed. Emotional overexcitability is manifested in the person's ability to form strong emotional attachments to others, and living

224

things and places. Also present with emotional overexcitability are: concern about death, strong affective memory, concern for others, empathy, exclusive relationships and feelings of loneliness. People with high levels of this OE often say they are "too emotional."

The level of development the individual reaches is dependent upon three factors. The first factor is the person's hereditary endowment, namely, the configuration of his overexcitabilities and other genetic inheritances. The second factor is the environment in which the individual lives and the extent to which it supports or impedes that individual's development, for example, family, school, community. The third factor consists of the individual's response to his or her situation—the decisions he or she makes in response to the life situation they find themselves in and the genetic heritage that they possess.

The third factor is only found at Level III or above, that is, persons at levels I and II are molded entirely by genetic and environmental factors. Only at Level III does the individual start to take hold of their situation (in an almost "existential" way) and make a conscious, self-determined choice as to how they will act.

Equipped with this brief overview of TPD (the theory of positive disintegration) let us now examine how some of these ideas might apply to examples from family life.

Multilevelness

In *Imaginary Groups*, I describe and explain how the levels of TPD can be seen as existing contemporaneously in all people and as dynamics in all groups. Further, individuals and groups are in constant tensional states as to which level (I through V) will dominate their ideation and behavior. These processes are manifested in families. Just as one may have a Level I individual (who has latent, or unconscious capacities for Levels II-V), so one may have a Level I family (with analogously latent capacities for levels II-V). Much of the drama of family life (if not all human life) can be understood as emanating from the dynamic tensions existing between the levels. Let us quickly examine some simple examples.

Level I Families
These families are very common in the popular media. Often the "gangster" family is a predominantly Level I phenomenon. "The Godfather," "The Sopranos," "Scarface," all depict families organized mostly around Level I ideals of brute force, lack of introspection and the ambivalence it might bring on, and primitive physicalistic motivations.

Interesting and poignant dynamisms are depicted in these narratives insofar as each of them involves elements of <u>positive maladjustment</u>.

In each narrative we do not find a completely smooth surface, nor the absolute opacity of Level I. There is an element of a key personality or an individual that is at odds with the reigning psychopathic paradigm, that is, someone is maladjusted, but in a positive way, in a way that betokens a higher level dynamic.

Michael Corleone (in "The Godfather III") tries to get out of the family business, but they "keep pulling him back." His wife has serious moral compunctions over the gangster way of life.

Tony Soprano has bad dreams, has anxiety attacks, and is seeing a psychotherapist. These are not Level I phenomena and their presence adds powerfully to the pathos of his personality. In addition, his wife, a classic Level II, whilst in denial much of the time, does have an occasional (Level III) pang of conscience.

Tony Montana (of "Scarface"), who so robustly exemplifies Level I behavior ("Say hello to my little friend."), shows distinct signs of multilevelness in his conflict over his ultimate refusal to kill children. (Interestingly, it is this refusal that leads to his death. Tony Montana died because of his conscience.) Tony's beautiful "say hello to the bad guy" speech, delivered to a bemused and anxious (yet admiring) restaurant crowd, is an eloquent indictment of the duplicity of Level II. Sadly for Tony he has nothing readily available to put in the place of the empty hole burned out by his skepticism. Tony Montana's wife loses herself, in a common Level II fashion, to drugs and alcohol. Unable to maintain a full-blown psychopathic lifestyle, she is, as yet, unable to move on to Levels III and IV and suffers unilevel disintegration—she goes to pieces in front of our eyes, as does Tony in the final scenes.

Not all Level I families are gangsters in the usual sense of the word. Many are simply unambivalent conformists that manage frequently to pass under the social radar. For example, World War II death camps were often run by people who went home after work was done and lived a harmonious "ordinary" life. Several of Hitler's henchmen came from quite ordinary, conventional, bourgeois backgrounds.

These examples should serve to remind us that "Level I" is not something always "out there." It is a potentiality available to all individuals and groups. It even, in its very simplicity, has a certain allure to it. When it is socially derogated, it is similarly tempting to see it, not as a potential in oneself, one's family or one's reference group, but as being "over there," in the other individual, family, group or nation. I like Freud's comment which gains so must more meaning in German or French): "La ou ça etait, le je doit être." ("There, where 'that' was, the "I" must be."

Level II Families

The Level II family dynamic can be described as much "storm and fury, signifying nothing." Families dominated by this dynamic will be confused, conflicted, ambivalent and ambitendent.

Examples from popular culture are again readily available. Most "soap operas" depict the level II dynamic. Characters shift and change values, even identities, "on a dime"; the conflict is never-ending and, at the end of the day, nothing has been accomplished or learned, it's back onto the same old treadmill. Love triangles, competition, fear of ostracism, anxiety over conformity and the panoply of Level II motivations hold sway.

Many classic examples of Level II families can be found in television situation comedies. Notable amongst them is "The Simpsons." Homer changes value systems sometimes several times in a sentence. Marge plays the role of conventional, caretaking woman, and Bart and Lisa both like to laugh at the violence of the "Itchy and Scratchy Show."

However, in the Simpsons we find significant multilevel tensions within individuals, within the family and between their family and others.

Lisa frequently speaks for Level III concerns and is positively maladjusted. She is concerned about justice, cruelty to animals, aesthetics, consciousness, meaning, and all the Level III dynamics are in evidence.

Bart sells his soul but has a moral crisis and each member (except Maggie?) has evidence of hierarchization, that is, of feeling that there are parts of themselves, dynamics, that are of greater worth than others.

I would argue that it is the presence of these multilevel dynamics that engages so many people and creates the sense of life we find in "The Simpsons."

Dabrowski pointed out that Level II was the most commonly occurring level; that it was a very vulnerable level, insofar as many people (and here, families) could not retain their integration throughout this stage; and that it required a tremendous amount of psychological energy to transform oneself (or by extension, one's family or group) into an individual, family or group functioning at Level III.

Thus, the Level II family dynamic will be very common, frequently riddled with problems of disintegration (addictions, neuroses, crises, psychoses, personality disorders), and requiring great and often uncomfortable effort to change.

Level III Families

Applying TPD to family systems, we arrive at the following formulations for the Level III family.

The Level III family will have tensions and breakdown phenomena, but these will be different from the Level II family insofar as they will be more multilevel. There will be a tension between what is in the family and what ought to be. This "ought to be" will not originate from social norms, or mores, "keeping up with the Joneses," or from a desire to conform. It will stem from an internal moral imperative, a "calling," as it were. Something stirs, either in the family as a whole, or perhaps in one or several members of the family. For example, a mother may feel a strong urge to help in the community; a daughter wishes to study religions to resolve a crisis of meaning; a family as a whole looks at its lifestyle and sees that much of it, although materially comfortable, is empty; an adolescent son challenges his parents' way of life and its many masks and feels profoundly alienated. In each of these tensional conflicts there is a clear opportunity for the family to grow, and the Level III family, since it has other elements of Level III functioning such as self-observation and autonomy, is sometimes able to capitalize on these tensions and mobilize their energy to potentiate growth.

This growth may not always be along tried and well-worn pathways, for Level III functioning necessarily involves positive maladjustment, where the individual (or social system or subsystem) does not fit into the status quo because it represents something of greater complexity than the status quo. The Level III family is either itself a "misfit" or has members that are "misfits." These "square pegs in round holes," however, are not rebels without causes, nor are they seeking attention or working towards other secondary gains emanating from gainsaying conventional wisdom. Upon inquiry, we find their maladjustment is, stands for, or is striving for something of a higher order of complexity. (For a further elaboration of the concept of complexity, you can go back into chapter one.)

Another aspect of Level III functioning is that of self-observation. A social system operating at Level III will examine its own process critically much in the way a Level III individual observes her/himself (or in the language of TPD, experiences "subject-object" in her/himself). This self-observation may show up in self-reflection, self-examination, journaling or an openness to examination by others.

As we can see, Level III is very rich in dynamisms and these will be reflected in the energy and complexity of the Level III family. A key difference between the Level II and the Level III family is that the Level III family, for all its confusion, is, deep down, headed somewhere in a fairly sustained fashion, while the Level II family is torn by ambivalence and ambitendency. This is a key difference, and especially important for anyone seeking to understand families to grasp.

Level IV Families

These families will be very rare. The Level IV family will be more organized, less chaotic and more directed in its activities in a sustained way toward its goals. This may sound like this family is a single-minded automaton, that, robot-like, achieves its aims. This is not the case. In fact, the robot family is more like the Level I family. The Level IV family is variegated and diverse on all levels. Individuals in it are internally complex and multifaceted and the group is comprised of different personalities. These differences are, however, accepted. The tensions created between the different parts and the different levels of complexity they embody potentiate dialog, discourse and, ultimately, growth. In fact, this "growth ethic" may be (explicitly or implicitly) part of the "family philosophy." This family is self-directed, autonomous and self-correcting. It is an open system, ever growing and facilitating the growth of all the parts of all its members.

Level V Families

Families operating at this level will be extremely rare; so rare, in fact, that they are more usually objects of imagination or visionary experience. The Level V family is perhaps rendered even rarer since so many sacred stories involve the transcendence or forsaking of family ties. Nonetheless, one can find examples of "holy families" or families of gods and demi-gods in various religions.

The story of Adam and Eve would be an example of a sacred couple, whilst the narratives of the Nativity, again from Christianity, depict a perfectly harmonious, inclusive, sacred family. The god-couple Zeus and Hera from ancient Greek religion depict a passionate and tempestuous pairing, while the Cahokian myth of Red Horn (of Mississippian, pre-Columbian culture) depicts sons rescuing and resurrecting their father.

Developmental Potential

A very important concept in TPD is "developmental potential." Developmental potential refers to the amount of available energy in the person or system that is particularly suited to the task of increased development through the Levels I, II, III, IV and V.

While energy for humans and social systems can be categorized into the five "overexcitabilites" (OEs): psychomotor, sensual, imaginational, intellectual and emotional), it is only the emotional OE that provides the kind of energy results in the increased complexity we see at the higher levels. It is therefore extremely important to know what happens to the emotional energy in a family, for not only will this give a reading of what level the family is operating on, but also of the developmental potential of the family, how far it can go.

The level of emotional OE is determined in part by genetics, in part by social and interpersonal experiences that can encourage or stunt emotional life, and in part by decisions made by individuals and groups. Especially important second factor determinants of emotional OE would be the amount of unworked trauma in an individual, family or social system. Unworked trauma creates a sort of psychic "scar tissue" that can dampen emotional responsiveness even in the most resilient person.

In addition, <u>secure</u> attachments in childhood are especially important in sustaining emotional OE. It is thus very important, from this perspective to support empathic attachments, if one wishes to promote development in the family.

By now, you are probably very aware that this book proposes that a family is a tensional field. Tensions operate between generations, between genders, roles, in the field of authority and between the conscious and unconscious, to mention just a few domains. This chapter opens up the possibility that there is another tensional field in the family—a tensional field between the different levels of Dabrowski's Theory of Positive Disintegration. These tensions exist within and between individuals. Each individual contains within them elements of each of Dabrowski's five levels. Some of these levels predominate and may exert hegemony and others may be virtually silenced, but there is always the potential for multilevel dialogue—this is Dabrowski's notion of <u>developmental potential</u>.

Similarly, multilevel tensions exist to a greater or lesser extent, and with greater or lesser degrees of consciousness between individuals in the family. Thus, an individual may, if they are sufficiently "multilevel," hear an array of voices inside her/himself, voices emanating from different parts of the self, at different levels of emotional development. And a family, too, may manifest a panoply of "voices" coming from different levels—the confident psychopathic voice of level I, the wavering, drifting voice of level II, the moral anguish of level III, the visionary inspiration, perhaps, of Level IV, and the ineffable mystery of Level V. The theory of positive disintegration thus offers another template, another useful map, to chart the complexities of the family

CASE EXAMPLE: The Perez Family

The Perez family, Mike, 47, Theresa, 46, and Tom, 17, come to counseling because of intractable problems at home. Tom, who is a gifted visual artist, has been very recalcitrant. His grades have slipped and his parents are concerned. When they attempt to control him, he rebels.

Mike is a successful philosophy professor at a local college and has written several books on ethics. In addition, he is a community activist, pressing for the rights of marginalized and under-represented. Theresa works as a social worker, helping the homeless. The family is comfortably-off economically and both Mike and Theresa are devoted to helping others, describing themselves as "old school liberals working off their middle class guilt."

Tom is very bright and verbally fluent. Although clearly possessing an independent spirit, he does not seem clear in his direction. He is quick to challenge the counselor's ideas and unwilling to see contradictions in his logic. He says he is made up of different people "assembled from different colonies," all going in different directions. His art expresses his many feeling: joy, despair, longing, rage and much of his work is "phantasmagoric." He has offers from several schools for scholarships, but seems at times to be unaware of what a great opportunity he has, almost negligent of his potential for success. And then, at other moments he evidences empathy, caring and gratitude for the self-same parents he was berating but a few minutes before.

Answer the following questions in an attempt to apply the Theory of Positive Disintegration (TPD) to this family.

1. *What levels are the family members at? What is your evidence?*

2. *What over excitabilities do you discern? How:*

3. *If you were to put this entire family at one of the TPD levels, which one would you select? Why?*

4. *How does TPD help explain what is happening in this family, especially with regard to Tom?*

5. *What consultation do you think a TPD-oriented counselor would give to this family? Does it seem like a good interpretation when compared with other frameworks such as those covered elsewhere in this book?*

CHAPTER 10
Play and the Family

Play is a serious business. It is widely known that play serves many functions. It helps take our minds off serious, stressful topics and gives relief to strain. At the same time, play can offer an avenue for resolving serious issues, for letting off steam safely or for thinking things through. Children love to play. When people suffer from emotional difficulties, one of the first things to suffer is the sense of play.

The very process of play, involving, as it does, symbolic activity and creativity, helps people see things in a new light. Play brings different interpretations to bear on phenomena. This very process of seeing things from a different point of view helps solve problems and gives relief and hope in difficult and even desperate situations.

When we look at the phenomenon of play in families we encounter a bewildering array--a complex field worthy of a book-length study. Some families are very unplayful and conduct their affairs in a very businesslike manner. In other families there is play but it might be very constrained and ritualized--the same board games are played, the same jokes are told. In some families play might be very competitive, while in others it might be aimed at making emotional contact. In yet other families play is active and open-ended, spontaneous and alive.

Another realm of family play has to do with who plays what with whom. Some families play as a whole group, while others might break into pairs, each playing specific games. In yet other families, members may play as isolates, on their own, or only with other groups, clubs or other families.

Activity 73:
In the following activity, think of two families you know and compare them in their modes of play, by answering the questions.

1. **How much does this family play?**

   Family A   **_Family B_**

2. **What does this family do for play? What games, sports, recreational activities?**

   Family A   **_Family B_**

3. **What are common themes of this play?**

   Family A   **_Family B_**

4. **Who plays with whom in this family?**

   Family A   **_Family B_**

234

5.   **What functions does play seem to serve in this family?**

Family A   *Family B*

6.   **What prescriptions (if any) would you make to each of these families with regard to play?**

Family A   *Family B*

Appendix A
Twelve-Week
Family Journal

Following is an outline for a weekly journal. Its purpose is to encourage further reflection and introspection. There are no right or wrong answers to the journal questions. Relax, write freely and spontaneously, using this journal as an exploratory tool. Try to write at least three sentences in response to each stimulus question. Also, always write a question to explore at the end. You may be surprised how this will stimulate your curiosity and discovery. If you want, you may share your journal responses with someone else to stimulate yet further reflection.

Journal

<u>*Week One*</u>

1. What do I hope for in family life?

2. What is important in families?

3. What are the primary tasks of a family?

4. Why are these tasks vital?

5. What questions do I have?

Week Two

1. What was a good movie I saw about families?

2. What was the lesson I learned from it?

3. One concept that we have covered in the course so far that seems to apply to this movie is...

4. One concept that we have not covered in the course so far that seems to be important in this movie is...

5. One question I have is...

Week Three

1. I interviewed someone from a different culture. The culture was

    _____.

2. One thing different in their culture from my culture regarding families was...

3. One thing that was similar to my culture regarding families was...

4. People choose whom they are going to marry in their culture by...

5. One question I am left with regarding culture is...

Week Four

1. A movie I saw which was about a family in a different culture was...

2. The important values in this family were...

3. The differences from my family and this family seemed to be...

4. The similarities between this family and the culture of my family were...

5. Questions I am left with are...

Week Five

1. Three roles that I have seen played in families are...(e.g., enabler, placator, rescuer, nurturer)

2. People played these roles by behaving in the following manner...

3. The impact the playing of these roles had on the family was...

4. If these individuals tried to change the role they played, then this is what frequently happened.

5. Questions I am left with are...

Week Six

1. When I interviewed someone as to how they will select a partner, I discovered...

2. When I select (or selected) a partner to create a family I will do so in the following manner...

3. The things that are essential ingredients of a successful relationship are...

4. Important barriers to intimacy that I have discovered are...

5. Questions I am left with are...

Week Seven

1. A relationship can be kept alive by...

2. When I interviewed or observed a couple that had been together a long time I learned...

3. When I think of what crises can do to relationships, I think...

4. When I interviewed or observed a couple that had children, I learned...

5. Questions I am left with are...

Week Eight

1. The most interesting thing I learned so far from this journal is...

And I intend to explore it further by...

Week Nine

1. Small babies seem to have these needs...

2. From my interviews and observations, small babies seem to impact families in the following ways...

3. Young children seem to have these needs...

4. And they seem to impact families in these ways...

5. Questions I still have are...

Week Ten

1. What does it mean to become a father?

2. What does it mean to become a mother?

3. How are your answers to questions one and two alike? Different?

4. What will be your strengths and weaknesses as a father or mother?

5. What questions still remain unanswered?

1. From my interview with an older person I found out this about being old...

2. What do you intend to be like when you are...

   Forty?

   Fifty?

   Seventy?

   Ninety?

Week Twelve

1. What role should sex play in a couple's relationship? How important is it?

2. How should the young be educated about sex?

3. How open should a couple's sexual relationship be?

4. What is your attitude towards your culture's attitudes towards sex?

5. What questions remain?

248

Summary of Journal

As I look at my journal I observe the following patterns in my responses and draw these conclusions...

Appendix B:
Project Outline: Our Family

For this project, you are asked to create, preferably as a group project, a family. The family can be of any size, with two or more members. Please feel free to include different sexual options, races, cultures and classes.

Create a folder that describes your family. You can use pictures, drawings and diagrams to ENLIVEN this project. The family, although imaginary, should feel real. This will be achieved if you integrate the things covered in this workbook and things you have observed and experienced. Following is a tentative outline for this project.

Our Family

1. Who are we? What type of family are we? (Nuclear, extended, blended, etc.)
2. Where do we live?
3. What do we do?
4. What are our dreams?
5. How are we functioning as a system? Are we an open or closed system? How are we doing financially, emotionally, educationally, etc.?
6. What life tasks do we face?
7. How are we handling those life tasks?
8. Do any of us have "symptoms"? If so, what are they and what function do they serve for the family?
9. How do the parents relate to one another? If single parent, how is he or she relating to others? What kind of love is in the family?
10. How do the children (or child) relate to others?
11. What lies in the future?
12. What unresolved issues still lie in the past?

13. Does this family need some help? If so, what kind of help?
14. What is our cultural environment like? How does it affect us? How do we affect it?

Present you family to a group. Have them react to it and analyze it along the lines laid out in this workbook. More likely than not your family will "spring into life." People should want to hear more, to "find out what happens next." Who knows, you may even be able to generate a plot for a great story for a film, play or television!

Bibliography

Here is a beginning list of books referred to in the text with some additions, should you wish to explore further.

Developmental Psychology

Blos, Peter. 1979. The Adolescent Passage. Madison, CT: I.U.P.

Bowlby, John. 1980. Loss. New York: Basic Books.

Dabrowski, K. 1970. Mental Growth through Positive Disintegration. London: Gryf.

Dabrowski, K. and M. Piechowski. 1977. Theory of Emotional Development. Oceanside, NY: Dabor.

Erikson, E. 1963. Childhood and Society. New York: Norton.

Greenspan, S. 1981. Psychopathology and Adaptation in Infancy and Early Childhood. Madison, CT: I.U.P.

Hazell, Clive. 2003. The Experience of Emptiness. Bloomington: Authorhouse.

Levinson, D. 1978. The Seasons of a Man's Life. New York: Knopf.

Levinson, D. 1997. The Seasons of a Woman's Life. New York: Ballantine.

Mahler, M. 1975. The Psychological Birth of the Human Infant. New York: Basic Books.

Sullivan, H.S. 1953. Interpersonal Theory of Psychiatry. New York: Norton.

Vaillant, George. 1977. Adaptation to Life. New York: Little Brown.

Gay, Lesbian Couples and Families

Cerbone, Armand. Coming Out as a Lifelong Task. (Unpublished presentation Illinois school for Professional Psychology, 1988)

Decker, B. 1983-84. "Counseling gay and lesbian couples," Journal of Social Work & Human Sexuality 2:39-52.

Isay, Richard. Being Homosexual. Farrar Strauss and Giroux, 1989.

Systems Theory

Bateson, G. 1972. Steps to an Ecology of Mind. San Francisco: Chandler Publishing.

Bertallanffy, L. von. 1968. General System Theory. New York: Braziller.

Laszlo, E. 1969. System, Structure and Experience. New York: Gordon and Breach.

Watzlawick, P., J.H. Beavin, and D.D. Jackson. 1967. Pragmatics of Human Communication. New York: Norton.

Group Psychology

Bion, W. 1961. Experiences in Groups. London: Tavistock.

Colman, A.D. and W.H. Bexton (eds.). 1975. Group Relations Reader. Washington, DC: A.K. Rice Institute.

Colman, A.D. and W.H. Geller. 1985. Group Relations Reader 2. Washington, DC: A.K. Rice Institute.

Hazell, Clive. 2005. Imaginary Groups. Bloomington: Authorhouse.

Psychological Type

Briggs Myers, Isabel. 1995. Gifts Differing: Understanding Personality Type. Davies-Black.

Family Therapy

Boscolo, Luigi. 1988. Milan systemic Family Therapy. New York: Harper Paperbacks.

Freud, S. (1914) 1958. Remembering, Repeating and Working Through Standard Edition 12:147-156. London: Hogarth Press.

McGoldrick, Monica. 1999. Genograms: Assessment and Intervention. New York: W.W. Norton.

Miller, A. 1981. Prisoners of Childhood. New York: Basic Books.

Minuchin, S. 1978. Psychosomatic Families. Harvard University Press.

Napier, August. 1988. The Family Crucible. New York: Harper.

Palazzoli, Mara Selvini, Luigi Boscolo, Gianfranco Cecchin, & Guiliana Prata. 1978/1994. Paradox and Counter-Paradox. Northvale, NJ: Jason Aronson.

Satir, V. 1964. Conjoint Family Therapy. Palo Alto: Science and Behavior Books.

Winnicott, D.W. 1971. Playing and Reality. New York: Basic Books.

Zuck, G.N. and I. Boszormenyi-Nagy. 1966. Family Therapy with Disturbed Families. Palo Alto: Science and Behavior Books.

Gender and Families

Chodorow, Nancy. 1989. Feminism and Psychoanalytic Theory. New Haven: Yale.

Gilligan, Carol. 1982. In a Different Voice. Harvard University Press.

Families

Laing, R.D. 1969. The Politics of the family and Other Essays. London: Tavistock Publications.

White, James M. 2005. Advancing Family Theories. Sage Publications.

Winnicott, D.W. 1964. The Child, the Family and the Outside World. New York: Pelican.

Winnicott, D.W. 1965. The Family and Individual Development. London: Tavistock Publications.

Videos, Movies

Constructing the Multigenerational Genogram: Exploring a Problem in Context. Topeka, KS: Menninger Video Productions.

The Joy Luck Club. Oliver Stone Production. Hollywood Pictures.

Not All Parents are Straight. The Cinema Guild.

Ordinary People. Paramount Pictures.

Scenes from a Marriage. 1973. Ingmar Bergman Film. Cinematograph AB.

Index